THE BLOSSOMS ARE GHOSTS AT THE WEDDING

SELECTED POEMS & ESSAYS

For David,
Fellow wonderer
in the salmon-haunted
place we "haunt."
Best
Fishes!
Tom Jay
12/06

TOM JAY

THE BLOSSOMS
ARE GHOSTS
AT THE WEDDING

SELECTED POEMS & ESSAYS

EMPTY BOWL

Empty Bowl is a division of Pleasure Boat Studio: A Literary Press
291 West 89th Street, New York, NY 10024

Printed in the U.S.A.

Grateful acknowledgement is made to the
University of Washington
for the use of Mary Randlett photographs.

Library of Congress Cataloging-in-Publication Data

Jay, Tom
The blossoms are ghosts
at the wedding: selected poems and essays / Tom Jay
p. cm
10-digit ISBN 1-929355-35-1
13-digit ISBN: 978-1-929355-35-8
Library of Congress Control Number: 2005939137

First Edition

EMPTY BOWL
423 THUNDER ROAD
Port Townsend, Washington 98368

Acknowledgments

Poems

Thanks to Copper Canyon Press for permission to reprint
from my book *Riverdogs* the following poems:
"Hunter's Song," "Stones," "Plainsong," "Masquer" and "Loki."

Thank to the editors of the *Montana Gothic* (Blackstone Press)
for permission to reprint "Snow";
and the editors of
AAG-AAG (Two Magpie Press)
for permission to reprint "The Leaper."

Essays

Thanks also to the following publications
(and their editors) in whose pages certain of my essays first appeared:

Upriver/Downriver: Words Bear Nature's Wisdom;
Land, Earth, Soil, Dirt; and Larva.

Environmental and Architectural Phenomenology Newsletter:
Culture Is A Mortal Nest.

Connotations (Journal of Island Institute): Familiar Music.

Alaska NW Books: Initiation and Homecoming from the book
Reaching Home Pacific Salmon Pacific People.

PUBLISHER'S ACKNOWLEDGEMENT

The publisher gratefully acknowledges the generous support of the Port Townsend
Arts Commission in helping to sponsor the production of this book.

Grateful thanks to Jerry Gorsline, Freeman House, Tim McNulty and
Connie Martin for hailing me into "reinhabitation"; to my wife Sara Mall
Johani, for her vital inspiring honesty; to Mike O'Connor and Wes Cecil
at Empty Bowl for their patience and care with my unruly text; to editor
poet Bill Bridges, whose classical perspective exorcized the book's pudgier
demons; and to Shannon Gentry, who composed these poems and essays
into a visually inviting book. Lastly, honor and thanks to photographer
Mary Randlett, the grand lady of Art and Nature in Washington State,
for use of two of her photographs in the book.

To my wife

Sara Mall Johani

MY SON

Dru Oja Jay

Contents

4 • CLUE

5 • FOCUS

6 • SURPRISE

EPILOGUE:

The Blossoms Are Ghosts at the Wedding

Selected Poems & Essays

PROLOGUE

Finding Moving Water

I LEARNED I COULD WATER WITCH from an old South Dakota farmer, Leonard Lechtenberg, who came to our green Western Washington valley after WWII to try dairy farming. I called him because he was recommended by my neighbors as a real dowser; he could find water. I called him up and asked if he would witch a well on our place. "I don't witch anymore. My heart isn't what it used to be; but come down to my place for a visit, and we'll find out if you can dowse. If you can, then you can witch your own well." Intrigued and skeptical, I accepted Leonard's offer and drove to his place to find out if I could dowse or water witch, whatever that meant. When I arrived, Leonard came out of his white clapboard farmhouse and waved at me to come up onto the porch. He was a black-haired gnomic man in his late sixties, stocky and almost plump, but powerful from years of hard work. He was naturally friendly, but not in a superficial way. From the beginning of our friendship, it was obvious that Leonard valued life's marrow more than its makeup.

After a brief chat and a survey of his farm and outbuildings from the porch, he invited me into the kitchen and produced a pair of 3/16" steel rods about 2 1/2' long, bent at right angles about six inches up their length. They looked like letter Ls. "These are witching rods. They're a great tool for finding veins of water if you're a dowser." He went on to explain that about one of four people can water witch to one degree or another. "It's like a birthmark, fingerprint or the color of your eyes, you can't learn or will to have such gifts, you are born with them." He showed me how to hold the rods, parallel to each other, the legs of the Ls level with the ground, with the feet of the Ls held vertically in the socket of the fist so the toes of the feet point down. The socket of the grip allowed the rods to pivot when you were over or on a vein of water. "I prefer the steel rods," he said. "They tell you more. You can trace a vein or tell when you hit a crossing vein. Some dowsers prefer a forked green willow branch. The branch is shaped like a Y. You grip the end portion of each arm of the Y with your palms up and with the single leg of the Y parallel to the ground. When you strike a vein, the leg points down. It feels like you've got a big fish on a strong line." In my experience, it feels like an invisible hand stronger than your own two is pulling the willow tip down into the ground. Sometimes this invisible force is strong enough to twist off the bark in your grip, or snap the arms of the *Y* because they are over bent by the pull of the hidden stream, the vein, as Leonard liked to call it.

"Either way, willow or steel, if you're a real water witch, you can't stop them from moving no matter how hard you try. Remember, dowsing is finding veins of live water, moving water. It's not the water, it's the water's motion you feel in the willow or steel." With that introduction, Leonard took me out onto the front porch and pointed to the access road that ran between the house and the barn. "Hold the rods as I showed you, tight, but don't put your thumbs on top of them. If you're a dowser, the rods will cross in front of you at a certain point down the road."

I walked down the steps toward the road, and Leonard went back inside. When I reached the road, I paused to check my grip on the rods, and turned to see Leonard in the kitchen window, waving me on. "Just walk slowly down the road," he called. "There's nothing to get; you either have it, or you don't!" So off I went, tentative and awkward, with the rods a little shaky in my uncertain shuffle. I wanted *it* to work, but didn't know what *it* was, so I couldn't fake it, or even encourage it. I walked on slowly, half-afraid, half-hoping, foolish and expectant. About twelve summer-dusty paces towards the barn, the rods began to turn inward, inexorably, determinedly, magnetically. Fascinated, I resisted the pull, squeezing the rods as tightly as I could, but true to Leonard's word they ignored my strain and crossed in eerie benediction.

"I thought it might work for you!" Leonard yelled from the kitchen window.
"Amen," I muttered to myself as I hurried back to the house. "Wow, it works," I said and laughed.
"Yeah, you passed the test," Leonard chuckled.
"The test?"

"Yes, some people want to fool with the rods to avoid embarrassment if they're not real dowsers. But I know from witching all over this place that the only moving water on this little road flows through a pipe buried right were you watched the rods cross. The pipe brings water from our well to the house."

"How did you know the water was moving?" I asked, still treading water in the little miracle welling up around me.

"While you were fiddling with your grip on the rods, I turned the sink water on. It's a foolproof test for would-be dowsers. Be careful, the rods pull strongly for you, so learn to temper your enthusiasm. You're not in charge, you're in touch."

Leonard then gave me a brief survey of folk learning around dowsing. He cautioned me to remain alert while witching and to check out willows and anthills in well-drained areas. Twenty-plus years of water witching have confirmed that folk learning. Ants and willows have a nearly unanimous predilection to locate their colonies and roots over veins of water. Science is only mildly curious about folklore, so I haven't uncovered any papers on ant or willow sensitivity to the electromagnetic dynamics of moving water. We do know that moving water is a "current" and creates a weak magnetic field by the motion of electrically charged water. Maybe the ants and willows have their own highly evolved dowsing abilities that help them locate and thrive over the veins that the rods reveal and wells confirm.

In his humble but telling remembrance of dowsing lore, Leonard mentioned that traditional peoples of northern Europe often kept a trout in their wells, in the belief that the water would be blessed with freshness. Science has recently discovered that pre-smolt salmon, fry and parr use the water-saturated, gravel-rich hyporrheic zone that flows next to, in and out of and about rivers and streams. The young salmon swim freely in the interstices of the perennially dark gravel and probably feed in its unknown ecology. In the hyporrheic zone the fry and parr are safe from larger predators who are too large to fit through the doors of that dark haven. I mentioned this finding to Dick Goin, a long time Olympic Peninsula salmon advocate and restoration volunteer. He said, "Oh yeah, I remember once we were digging gravel to supplement flood-scoured spawning beds. Our pit was at least twenty feet from the main channel and, you know, it wasn't long before we began to see young salmon that had followed the seep into our temporary gravel pit." It's not unlikely that European "well trout" were salmon fry that preferred the safe waters and easy food of the well to the chain mail gravel they used as refuge. No doubt many of them stayed too long and grew too large to slip through to the larger stream when the ocean called. They became well-locked salmon, virgin queens trapped in the upside down drowned towers of the underworld of springs and spirits. Folkloric witness and scientific fact, the blossoms are ghosts at the wedding.

My research reveals that Celtic mythology celebrated sacred wells wherein the Salmon of Wisdom dwelled. Pre-Christian Ireland had numerous wells haunted by sacred trout or salmon until the Christian church re-blessed them all with saints' names, and they became outposts of an alien lord's grace, rather than the mysterious blood of the local earth, the milk of the ancient goddess of creation.

Leonard told me to practice witching known wells, "to refine your feel," he said. He explained *bobbing*, witching for depth. The technique requires the dowser to hold the end of a 5-6' steel or willow rod over the found vein and touch the bobbing rod to that spot, then lift the wand slowly until level with the ground, at which moment the rod will begin to *bob*: bouncing up and down over the vein. The dowser counts these bobs, and uses the count to learn the depth of the well. By bobbing known wells, the water witch learns to calibrate his or her bob. My bob is a simple one-foot to the bob.

Leonard also showed me the rudiments of tracing a vein. Once the rods cross over a vein, you stand directly over that spot with the rods crossed, then, dropping your arms to your sides, you turn 90 degrees left or right and raise the rods, holding them parallel in front of you as before. If they stay parallel, you're in the flow, and can trace the vein by walking slowly forward, watching the rods and changing direction to keep them parallel over the flow. You wobble slightly side to side as you follow the vein's meander beneath the earth's mute forms. You follow a vein for two reasons: maybe there is an easier place to drill, and perhaps you'll hit a cross vein, increasing chances for more well capacity. When you hit a cross-vein, the rods will open outwards as if in welcome. When you bob the cross vein, the bobbing wand will hitch and circle once or twice at the shallow vein before continuing the count to the deeper water. Whether you use the steel rods or supple forked willow, water witching works. At least three quarters of the several wells I've witched over the years have come in at the indicated spot and within seven feet of the bobbed depth. When the witching hasn't worked, either the well driller moved the rig off the spot, or more interestingly, the well log reveals gravelly or sandy substrate that once bore water, but is no longer wet. It seems rocks may remember water flow, who knows? Dowsing has nothing to do with my talents, intentions or intelligence; it is nothing to be proud of, but a gift to be grateful for, like fine sight or being able to sing in key.

Since that day on Leonard's road, the ground beneath my feet has become a different creature. A well is now a noun and a verb. It is no longer a hole in the earth to mine water. It is a reverberation, a window, a womb, a breast, a liquid locus of belonging where the wet sun-stilled mystery of the world rises to refresh us. We are glints of light in the moon-knotted lace of water that ensouls the land. The blossoms are ghosts at the wedding.

Like writing, dowsing is a profound refreshment for me. Neither work nor play, it is a kind of serious dreaming proved finally at the point of a stone-tempered drill or ballpoint pen. Hydromancy is similar to poetry in that, like hidden, moving water, you have to risk and dig to enjoy its refreshment. You have to work slowly, attentively, to reveal if the current's call is an inspiration or an illusion, a weak shallow vein or a potential artesian. Sometimes you're stumbling through a blackberry-cursed clear-cut and sometimes you're strolling in the shaded sanctity of an ancient forest. (It's no accident that *speech* is from an Indo-European root *sper* that gives us sprinkle, sparkle, sperm, among other wet familiars. Similarly, *rhyme* and *rhythm* spring from another Indo-European root *sreu* to flow, which gives us stream and rheostat among others. The basic notion is current.) For more than twenty years I have witched the occasional well for friends and neighbors. I don't charge, few dowsers do. "How could you charge for the color of your eyes?" warned Leonard. Dowsing's traditional simple implements invite the ancient genius of our bodies' notions to trace the subtle snake of living water in the earth's heat-cracked, bone-littered heart. Likewise, the well-grounded living word and the subtle ancient echoes of daily conversation locate and instruct the poet's rainy inspiration.

The blossoms are ghosts at the wedding. Our world is haunted by water. But besides the stone-breaking insinuations the dowser divines, we are part of and prey to water's slippery pandemonium—in rills, frosts, fogs, seas, mists, waves, springs, clouds, aegirs, in tides, in blood and bodies, in lakes, ponds, floods and drenching rain. Water haunts life inside and out; we die without its grace. We are its clay-footed, star-eyed offspring, ocean's orphans upright in the wind. Our water-born awareness bends to the well-spoken word the way the willow branch twists and dives in my work-hardened hands. Both currents are real as rain. We have only the death-stirred crucible of our hearts to receive their vivid whispered renewals. The water-mothered weather of this mortal world and the braided babble of songs and cries that edge and animate our mortal masks are the threads that spin our fate. The dowser's witness and a breathing poem are forms of pledge, an inner weather wherein the leaf-voiced wind runs ahead, alone and empty handed to announce the arrival of the soulful, salmon-eyed rain. The blossoms are ghosts at the wedding.

Crossing Hood Canal Bridge

It was clear.
A cat's eye day.
An old farmer friend and I
had just dropped the winter's pigs
off to the butcher.
On the way home we talked,
he pointed to the land around us
and said:

> "When I first came here, it was terrible.
> The loggers had been everywhere, ruined
> trees, nothing held the ground water, wells
> went dry. You could buy land for fifty cents
> an acre. Ruined. Where I came from
> trees are rare, still the greenness
> of this place brought me back."

and I thought:

> "They learned late, the farmers,
> the loggers, the highway builders.
> Men who gloried in their youthful
> strength and saw too late the ruined
> forest, the barren ground, the preposterous
> roads. It is a bitter old age for
> them, tuneless and grim. They know
> they ruined the bell they rang
> so fiercely."

And yet:

> A few men always know. My friend told of a harvest time
> long ago on the high plains,
> when his father, seeing another man
> mistreat his own horse,
> whipped the miscreant to his knees
> with a dead black snake.

1 • HOME

Our word *home* blossoms from the Indo-European root *kei* ("to lie down, to be recumbent"). This root nourishes the words civic, city, hamlet, cemetery and Shiva, among others. In Old English it appears as *ham* ("home, a house with land"). *Ham* has a derivative *ham-etan* ("to house"), which is related to Old Norse *heimta* ("to bring cattle home from pasture"), whence the Old French word *hanter* ("to dwell in, to frequent"). *Hanter* becomes English ("to haunt"). Home is a place wherein we rest, dream, and return. Home is the familiar haunt, the grave dwelling of concordant dreams.

A Slip of Silver

A luminous dream cradled in the muffled
rattle of creek-worried stones, an eyelit shadow
coiled in the fertile mercy of my egg...soon I will
swim up sleek into the sun dappled wake of water
and flash, a slip of silver in the braided babble
of my sea-mad stream.

Who are we?

My salt-wise soul, grown nimble and dark
with blood in the treacherous feed of the sea, gyres
the ocean's pilgrim-haunted swell and in the third summer
of its winding catches,
like an orphan startled by
his mother's eyes, the scent of the grave-strong
stones of home and dashes in water-shattered
moonlight back into the rainy wealth of his nativity.
Hook-nosed, bruised, gravid tatter-finned dragon of the
brook, my canny strength gone into milt or eggs, spent
like a dying man's last tithe, I cast my life back to the
endless roil of stones and drift away, a dazed
feast for a tumult of hunger, my ruined beauty
borne on in every body, deepening the inevitable
soil and its fateful dream of trees.

Who are we?

Throne Poem

Time is a hive
of incredible bees;
working the world;
enjoying and nurturing
its star-fed strength.
We are, each one,
the hive's own queen.

Speckled Dream

I went to the sea
for myself.
She fed me health,
new legs,
perhaps a speckled dream
to wrestle in the night.

Pond

Still water seems to see.
Note the pond's alder-lashed eye
unblinking,
even in the ice-blind
gray of winter.

Faithful pupil focuses the wind-stirred,
star-haunted crucible of sky
remembers each winding season
in its dream-dark, water-sifted reverie.
The long patient wait of water
presses the weather-ciphered pages of its text:
blossom, pollen, seed and bone,
blossom, pollen, seed and bone.

Hunter's Song

Striking,
stricken.
An eagle with a fish too big to lift,
I answer from my place.

Stones

Stones,
time's hard skulls,
blind mutes,
polished frozen loaves of fire.
Stones,
mountains down on their luck,
mystic dice
slow rolling
in the earth's incredible dream.

Landscape

House-sized rocks
moved hundreds of miles
by rivers of ice....

Fire-tempered trees
nursed skyward
by the bones of ocean-blessed fish...

A thousand songs
wait unquickened
in the rain and wind.

Storm

All night the storm
cracked and hissed in the treetops.
The old green gods
throw off their dark disguises
and dance in the fierce fault of night and day,
until the silent morning sun calls them home
behind their masks of cloud, wood and stone.
Only the broken fir limbs
and the scattered cone purses
recall their wanton revels.

2 • HAG

Hag derives from old Germanic words for hedge or woods. A hag is the woman on the other side of the Hawthorne hedge, a woman of the woods, a wild woman, untamed.

Remember kissing your grandmother, the soft papery flesh of her cheek scenting of faraway wild roses or the faint autumnal creek-borne air over the tawny water of a pond…?

Remember how her body seemed a thin weathered tent sheltering her passionate storied bones…?

Remember collecting spawned-out kelts, their familiar corporal feast drug up and ravished on the slippery bank by otter and coon or abandoned silt-shrouded and drowned gray in the quiescent braided eddies of the stream …?

Remember sawing off their love-bruised heads and bagging their distant stares in ziplocks, writing their runny numbers in the unfathomable calculus of the rain…?

Remember teasing out the telltale pearly otolith necklaces from the eye-watering corruption of their minds, bony postcards from the nether-world…?

Remember standing helpless as extras in the operatic road-killing storm while the creek roars, a torrential dragon snaking oblivious to the sea…?

Remember how the same stream giggles like an enchanted child in September's balmy sun…?

Remember the health-dark flash of the smolt as they leave the net pen nursery and how the redwing blackbird bells the wobbly air of spring; how the shadow- shy green heron rises startled and ghostly from the amber stillness of the winter pond…?

Embracing all this we quench a thirst that withers most and in its refreshment trace our sovereignty in this fitful world for what it is, an old woman's wedding gift.

INITIATION

YEARS AGO I WORKED AS A BOAT PULLER on a trawler fishing the Fairweather grounds, west of Glacier Bay, Alaska. We were newcomers to Alaska. The skipper, Larry Scoville, was an old friend and seasoned Northern California troller. We were fishing a new boat with a new diesel, so Larry and I spent a few days in the fjords and passes around Elfin Cove rehearsing the gear, the boat and crew. We were testing FV *Sinara* for any quirky motions, vibrations or noises that might spook the wily salmon. Larry watched my side of the boat, counting the fish caught, and warned me if the salmon didn't like my smell I'd have to wear gloves when I baited leaders or changed "hoochy" lures. The *Sinara* worked, and I was confirmed a bare-handed boat puller. We caught a scatter of silvers and kings, and headed for the Fairweather grounds and the chance to catch some big king salmon.

The second day on the grounds, Larry had us fishing frenetically on a school of stout king salmon. In the midst of the blood-slippery melee, Larry called me to bring the landing net to his side of the boat. He was working a tremendous king salmon on a rubber snubber we called the kill line, and gave me instructions on how to approach the salmon with the net, because it would have been foolish to land such a large salmon with a gaff. It was the biggest king I had seen that summer, slab-sided, thick-bodied and five feet long, perhaps a 100-pounder. As I brought the net behind and under it, it began to swim away not fast, but steadily, like a draft animal pulling a heavy load. The kill line went taut and the 100-pound test line snapped as the great fish flashed out of sight. This story is a reminder that the salmon is free and that the musings that follow are only lines and hooks that hold it momentarily.

The season was a bust. The silvers were late and the kings, hit or miss, so I quit before the season ended and went south to Seattle to study and work. It was seven years before I saw another free salmon. Settled with my family in the Olympic Peninsula community of Chimacum, Washington, one frosty winter evening I walked to the modest alder-lined creek that winds through the pasture south of our place. Lost in the icy stillness, I was startled by a sudden, staccato splashing. Whatever it was gathered its energy in quiet, then burst forward again, closer, moving up the creek. I crept to the cattle bridge to glimpse this night visitor.

In the ice-blue light of winter, a salmon flourished, dorsal fin and back just breaking the easy iridescent ripples of the stream. Another dark sparkling dash and it was below me in a log-dammed pool. It was a large wild male coho, smoky red and silver in his spawning regalia. Migrating at night while hunters dream, the salmon had followed the scent of this creek home, a pilgrimage repeated faithfully by his ancestors since the last ice age.

Witnessing the homecoming of this ancient being, the salmon, so precise, practiced and generous in his longing, quickened my own sense of homecoming. I felt lost and found at the same time squinting into the polished darkness of the water, afraid to lose that timely guide. In that numinous moment on the bridge, salmon became my teacher. He has kindled and animated my curiosity and I have followed him into the haunted waters of watersheds and folklore. Since that night on the bridge, salmon have been swimming in my dreams.

Salmon are born in brooks, creeks, rills the headwaters of greater streams. They run to the sea for a miraculous sojourn. Feasting, their flesh reddens in the richness of the sea. Mature, they awaken to the call of their natal waters, and follow clues subtle and disparate as magnetic fields and the bouquet of stones to the streams of their birth to spawn and die. Loving and dying in home ground is a primordial urge. Salmon embody this for us, our own loving deaths at home in the world. Salmon dwell in two places at once, in our hearts and in the waters, and they know the way home.

Once nearly every watershed around the North Pacific Rim, from San Diego, California to Kyushu Island in southern Japan, supported one or more runs of Pacific salmon (king, sockeye, pink, chum, coho, steelhead, masu, and amago). Each run or stock of salmon fits itself over eons to local conditions, its adaptability tempered by ice ages, floods and droughts. The vital beauty of salmon has been shaped by the infinite refinements of necessity. The salmon's genius is in making friends with fate. The king salmon of the Elwha River in Washington, for example, have evolved to enormous size, up to six feet and 100 pounds, because females must be powerful enough to excavate spawning beds (redds) below the scour depth of this steep and highly energized river.

The myriad life histories and the fine and grand morphological differences the salmon have evolved over thousands of years might be imagined as embodiments of watershed character—the salmon an expression, a vernacular of the watershed. Logically and poetically, the salmon are the soul of the watershed, its glory. Salmon are, as the salmon restoration herald, Freeman House, announced thirty years ago, the totem of the North Pacific Rim. Freeman was restating a wisdom familiar to the indigenous peoples of the North Pacific Rim. The Yurok of California and the Ainu of Japan, while separated by thousands of miles of ocean, celebrated the salmon as a vital element of their cosmos. In many regions human culture coevolved with the salmon, because both species—*Homo sapiens and Oncorhynchus*—were recolonizing the post-glacial barrens at the same time.

In the rub of weather and landscape, Native peoples and salmon adapted behaviors to fit local conditions. As the glaciers retreated, strays from re-fugia salmon populations began to probe the meltwater rivers and streams that drained the tundra landscapes of the glacial wake. Periodic heavy gla-cial outwash could wipe out generations of salmon and limit the success of salmon forays into new watersheds. While the persistent salmon fertilized the raw waters of glacial watersheds, plant communities, migrating north and south from unglaciated botanical preserves, were gradually reestab-lishing conifers in the post-glacial landscape. It was this "conspiracy" of salmon and trees that transformed and stabilized the watersheds of the North Pacific.

Large conifers provided shade, stream structure and a detritus-based aquatic food chain that nurtured the various species of Pacific salmon. Salmon runs moved tons of sediment downstream and helped stabilize river channels. Salmon also returned ocean-gathered nutrients to the rain-leached and gla-cially plowed soils of much of the North Pacific. As spawning and spawned-out salmon were retrieved from streams by bear, otter, eagle, raven and oth-ers, their nutrients were distributed throughout the forest.

A local forester once took me to a gargantuan grandmother fir, still regal in a mature second-growth forest. Four large people holding hands could barely encircle its girth. Its wind-blasted top was crowned with an active osprey nest. While we all craned our necks to view the nest, the forester pointed to the foot of the tree and asked what we saw. Around the base of the tree were tracks and scat of all kinds: coyote, raccoon, bear, deer, squirrel. "You see," he said, "the young osprey are much like our children when they dump their oatmeal off the high chair, except here the dropped food (salmon) is mopped up by a host of creatures, even deer and squirrel, who nibble the bones for calcium." This great fir, miles from any salmon creek, was a distribution point for forest nutrients. By dropping salmon from the treetops, the osprey were providing a welcome feast for the savvy creatures below. Seen in this light, salmon are a current between the forest and the sea. Salmon are sea-bright silver shuttles weaving the rain-green world of the temperate Pacific watersheds.

About 5,000 years ago, when salmon were established and abundant, Native peoples would move seasonally to fishing camps along streams and feast. But when the runs were over, the people had to move on after other food, for they had yet to develop food preservation techniques to take full advantage of the salmon bounty. Once Native peoples mastered salmon food preservation, they settled in permanent villages near preferred fishing sites. They learned through over-harvest and calamity-induced famine to manage the salmon resource at maximum sustainable yield. Pre-contact native cultures were probably harvesting more salmon than nineteenth- and twentieth-century industrial fisheries. Some researchers estimate that the Native harvest of salmon in the Pacific Northwest had been reduced ninefold before the large influx of European pioneers. The thundering "walk-across" runs reported by early European settlers were likely the result of tribal populations being decimated by the epidemics and whiskey that announced European eminence.

In pre-contact times, by working diligently during the salmon season, a family could store in a few months enough fish to meet its basic food requirements for a year. Of course there were supplemental foods—deer, seal, whale, fowl, shellfish, and plants, berries and seaweed—but the fundamental food resource was salmon. It was the axis of their economy and the hub of their culture. The salmon's abundance gave early peoples leisure, the time to develop the refined and distinct cultures of the North Pacific Coast.

Given their long association with salmon and its importance to them, it is no wonder that original peoples developed a deep and coherent connection to salmon. We moderns love salmon; it is the choice food of our region. But to the first peoples of the North Pacific, salmon was not merely food, it was energy. It was not energy in our sense of Btu's or calories, but was what William Blake meant when he said energy is eternal delight. Native peoples' close relations with salmon had worn through to a kind of intuitive essence: the salmon was the animate representative of greater powers, a fellow being and fateful herald of an *aweful* universe.

Many peoples of the North Pacific honored the salmon on its yearly return home. They imagined salmon as a representative of the other side, the world where the powers of creation reside. To the Ainu, Gilyak and Chukchi of Northeast Asia, the salmon was representative of the sea spirit. To the tribes of the Northwest Coast, it was a supernatural human being whose village was in the sea and who put on the salmon disguise as a gift to honor the respect the local people showed the salmon people.

In the Native cosmos, salmon can choose to present themselves in abundance or not at all. This vision required special treatment for the salmon. When the S'Klallam of Beecher Bay, British Columbia, caught the first sockeye salmon, little children sprinkled their hair with sacred white eagle down, painted their faces and put on white blankets. They met the canoe and carried the first salmon in their arms as if it were an infant. An older woman cleaned the fish with a mussel-shell knife, after which the flesh was boiled and given to the children to eat. To the S'Klallam, the sockeye is a person and deserves careful treatment. Versions of the first salmon ceremony were practiced by Native peoples from California to Japan. The salmon was treated as a respected guest before it was eaten, so that when the salmon spirits returned to their watery villages they would report that their gifts had been honorably received.

For the first people of the North Pacific, the salmon was a gift from hidden but prescient powers. The salmon was sacramental food, and the proper attitude was to feast on its energy in gratitude and repay its generosity by respectful treatment. You couldn't have your cake unless you ate it in gratitude. The Chukchi of Kamchatka ate the first salmon caught themselves; they wouldn't sell it to their Russian masters. You can't have your cake and sell it, too. The Gilyak of Sakhalin Island, north of Hokkaido, Japan, had a special language for speaking to salmon and other game. The Koryak of Siberia had a story called "Fish Woman" in which a man marries a fish woman, and though she is loving and patient, the mistreatment she receives in his house causes her to leave and take her relatives with her. This story echoes a Northwest Coast Tsimshian tale wherein a man mistreats his wife, "Salmon Woman," who returns to the sea with her silvery familiars. Native relations with the salmon resource required the same care, responsibility and attention as marriage, all qualities crucial to survival.

In the autumn, the Ainu of Japan watched for the magnolia leaves to fall because this presaged the arrival of the chum salmon. When they took the first salmon from the river, they passed it through a special game window in their house and honored the salmon ritually in front of the hearth fire. In their world, fire could see and report back to the supernatural world the hospitable treatment of the salmon. The Ainu also had a ceremony to bid the salmon spirits farewell when, in their human form, they paddled their canoes back to their homes in the supernatural world.

These beliefs are a deep recognition and affirmation of the place of the human imagination in nature. Native legend is a well-spoken alchemy of soul and landscape, each story informed by a thousand tellings. The wisdom of Native peoples is to live in and husband a world wherein nature and its beings hold humans responsible for their actions.

I once swam down Washington's Duckabush River in wet suit and mask. It was during the dog salmon run and there was a flood of fish in the river. The current ran both ways that day. Halfway down the river I floated over a deep pool where an eddy had piled a pyramid of golden alder leaves. Further on, resting in the shallows and musing on what I'd seen, I noticed a shape move behind a submerged snag. It was a large male dog salmon, splotchy gray and yellow with faint copper tiger stripes; spawned out but alive in his eyes. I dove and glided toward him until we were a foot apart. I looked into his eye. He saw me but did not move. I was just another river shadow, an aspect of his dying. He was crossing over to the other side, watershed specter feeding the firs, subterranean sometime king, tree-born elder, tutor.

Familiar Music: Reinhabiting Language

My father, Layton Leroy Jay, was a miner in his youth. He worked in the lead and silver mines of Northern Utah. He "mucked" and shoveled his way through college, a year in the mines, a year in school. He could still outlast me with a shovel well into his sixties. My father was proud of his hard won education and encouraged a large and practiced vocabulary as proof of its discipline. Whenever I had a question about word usage he sent me to the giant anvil of a Webster that doubled as a flower press in the corner of our living room. It was a proud day for me when I could finally carry it to the privacy of my room. From our first encounter the dictionary was a source of wonder and reverie for me. In its cogent dream I discovered that language is a vital reality and that each word preserves and expresses a perception, a subtly consecrated and traditional moment in the articulate mystery we call life.

Language called me like a secret ally from a forest's shade and I found myself a fledgling sparrow in its weathered wealth. I read the dictionary for pleasure, marveling at the depth, nuance and diversity of the language I spoke. I studied Latin because it amplified and inflected many of the words we breathe into English each day. Language is still numinous territory for me and perusing a well-conceived dictionary is like sneaking into a darkened ancient church and daydreaming in its rainbowed holy shade. But it wasn't until my thirties that my calling to language was confirmed by a startling lexical epiphany.

I was thirty-six years old, an egotistic, almost young poet whose first poems had been published a few years earlier. Still hungry for praise I was trying to write poems, force poems, establish a reputation. But inspiration had abandoned me, evaporated like the fey glimmer of a tree in summer mist. The poems soured; became tacky constructs of sentiment, murky perception and waning wit. The poems were loud, Hawaiian shirts of poems without a hint of the silence that frames and sustains an original poem. I hadn't learned that poems are not made, they're born and raised, like orphans left crying at your door.

> *Original* inherits its verbal means from Latin *origo* ("source, spring"). The root image in *original* is water rising out of the earth, water struck from stone.

One spring day, confused and parched in the untimely drought of my dilemma, surrounded by crumpled scraps of paper, I confronted my language romance with this complaint: "Okay. These poems are pretentious and contrived, muse-less; so if the muse is real, tell me her name." I waited attentively in the wisp of my innocence, pen in hand, expectant. But no answer arrived and after a while spring's green spell subverted my vigil and I began to doodle and daydream, absent-minded in the verdant charm of the day.

I woke from my reverie an hour later and there among the florid mazes, architectural cartoons and fantastic geometry of my doodles was a single word scribbled unawares: *kuma*...off I went to my trust of dictionaries. *Kuma.* I looked for her in three sources—no help. Still a persistent voice watered my hope, "Maybe you spelled it wrong. Maybe kuma is an old word." So I tried again and found it under cyme in *Partridge's Origins* (a short etymological dictionary of modern English.) A *cyme* is an inflorescence, a young cabbage sprout, the decoration atop a Greek column. *Cyme's* root is Greek Kuma, ("a wave, a sprout, anything swollen"). Kuma is from the Greek verb *Kuein* ("to be pregnant"). I had my answer. One fair name for the muse is *Kuma,* a swollen wave, a sprout, a form generated in the great dream of the somnambulant sea, headed your way, headed my way. She announces herself with a whispered roar and breaks radiantly on our peculiar shores. Since that spring day I seriously attend any word or phrase that wells up in my mind.

That daydream taught me that one had only to absent the personal mind as agent, yet maintain it as disciplined witness and the deep intelligence of language might emerge. In that moment I learned the truth of the muse: that inspired language, spoken or written, originates not in personal cleverness but in the fertility of language itself. The uncanny surprises in the realm of language—"Freudian" slips, unexpected eloquence, hot-cross puns and poems born fully grown and dancing—are the natural blossoming of language's richness, the dark prescient wisdom of its ancient and mortally tested soul. The essential Eros of language is evident in the way we name the details of our daily work. The logger keeps an eye out for a widow maker, a loose and potentially dangerous branch perched in the tree he's felling. The salmon troller arranges her "hoochies"—luminous, googly-eyed imitation squid—neatly by the hydraulic gurdies she works so deftly, bouncing her heavy lead on the sea bottom, luring king salmon to strike. Language's vitality metaphors the world it attends. It is the spoken music of our animate, many-weathered and deep-soiled home.

About that time I became curious as to the nature of my local community and began to study ecology. Kuma's revelation that language is inherently and naturally alive resounded deeply with ecology's essential metaphors: community, co-evolution, locality and cycles. I began to imagine language as an ecology, as vivid and nuanced as a forest. I came to see English as an atmosphere, a climate, the deft, rich warp and weft of human witness. Language is a locale, a temporal location and soulful place wherein we make love, dream and die. We wrap ourselves in the familiar roll of its weather, we are its water.

> *Ecology* from Greek *oikos* ("home, dwelling place") and *logos* ("talking, logic, legend"), hence *ecology* ("the home story, home legend, home logic").

A notable concept in ecology is the notion of the edge. When two ecosystems meet, say the forest and prairie, a border of rich diversity and fertility precipitates between them, a place of increased imagination. The evolved, well practiced narratives—*oikos* ("stories")—of the two systems are mixed in a terminus, a verge of opportunity and peril. Our ancestors probably became bi-pedal and brainy in the fertile shift of the tropical forest and savannah verge. In function and practice language is more truly an edge ecology, a fertile border, a vibrant brood between the human soul and the natural world.

Language is metaphoric. It bears our attention beyond ourselves towards the world. In speech we meet and affirm the gritty mystery of being, and in that affirmation, language is a lively marriage of soul and cosmos. Language is naturally erotic, a nearly forgotten form of love, the caress of shaped breath. Denied its connection, its Eros, we wither in the alienated self-reflection of jargons. I see language as the spoken record of myriad meetings between humans and the cosmos, two natures woven into wisdom, a fertile border, a skin with soul on either side, a semi-permeable membrane, a go-between, a Janus-headed Robin Hood, mercurial, tricky and true, inside out a glove that fits either hand…weird old words.

Language has a life of its own, and words, contrary to contemporary percepts, are not so much tools as organisms, evolved symbiots living in the breathed edge between our psyches and creation. Rather than sharpening, oiling and polishing our terms we do better to respect our words as if they were plants and animals; attend their generosity and wisdom rather than manipulate their resource. We might re-imagine ourselves as hunter-gatherers in the ecology of language rather than engineers, mechanics or arrogant tinkers of its raw material. Words are more like game trails than machetes. Our word *term* once meant ("border"). A term is where we meet the world. The spoken or written word is the articulation of that meeting, the I-Thou joinery, its joint. Speaking and listening well allows insight to the informed silence of the other side, becomes a room where the other may enter. Language is the habitat of revelation, yet language will lie if forced to do our bidding. But if we honor its lore, the lasting track of its vitality, it will invite us to speak. *Speak* shares an Indo-European root, *sphareg* ("to swell, teem, abound") with ("spark, spore, sprinkle, sparkle, disperse, sperm"). Language is a fertile liquid.

But language not only sparks and spores, is not only a seminal presence; it is also a soil, an archaeology, a ghostly host to its own story. Calvin Watkins, a noted philologist, was able to reimagine and locate a creditable homeland for our Indo-European ancestors by simply listing the oldest root words in the Indo-European family of language and cross referencing the list with the findings of paleo-ecology in Eurasia. The list included root words for *bear, mouse, hornet, beech tree, salmon* and others and tentatively placed our ancestral home west of the Urals and north of the Black Sea in the ancient forest that covered what is now Eastern Russia. Languages evolve, adapt and borrow; words have lineages and genealogies. Linguists can deconstruct a modern term and identify its ancestor word and the period when it began its haunt of the habitat we call English.

Every language on the planet has an age. English is relatively young, almost nine hundred years old, the child of a spear point wedding between Norman French and Anglo-Saxon. Some languages are thousands of years old: Irish, German, Greek, and Persian. Some are tens of thousands of years old; Kung, Ainu, Basque and the Aboriginal languages of Australia and the Americas.

Each language has been lorically shaped by its home-scape. Languages live and die, lasting as long as their lore is true. According to the linguist Michael Krause, minority languages in the English language sphere face a 90 percent extinction rate between now and sometime in the next century.

> *Loric*—from Old English Laeran ("to teach, to lead someone on their way"). *Laeran* is akin to Old English. *Laest* ("track") which gives us last ("what endures, a remaining way, a path that lasts"). Lore is a lasting, well worn track, the way of the ancestors, where your foot touches the ground.

"Therefore, in these days when a major problem is the growth of an originally Anglo-American, but now genuine global, monoculture that reduces everything to the level of the most mind-numbing stupendous boredom, I would think that the preservation of minority languages like Irish, with their unique and unrepeatable ways of looking at the world, would be as important for human beings as the preservation of the remaining tropical rainforest is for biological diversity." Diversity is the wealth of eco-systems and culture, the wealth time and life have heaped upon our shore, cumulative, Kuma again, gracing the shore of our awareness.

> *Articulation* shares the Latin root *artus* ("joint with art, arthritis, artificial") and ("inert not-jointed"), hence ("unable to move").

Languages offer unique perspectives on the world, different articulations of reality. Twenty years ago I had a conversation with a young friend named Ben. When Ben was five or six years old his family moved to the South Pacific island of Woleai. His parents had contracted to teach English as a second language to the people of Woleai. Ben soon became fluent in Woleain and entered the culture it centered. For eight years Ben spoke English with his parents and Woleain with everyone else. I once asked him if he believed in ghosts. "When I speak English, I don't, " he replied. "What do you mean?" I asked. "Well," he answered, "When I speak Woleain on Woleai I see them." Language in synch with a landscape ripe with ancestral mythology quickens a cultured, shared reality where the storied richness of the past animates and accents the present moment.

The Irish poetess, Nuala Ni Dhomhnaill, makes a similar point. "Irish is a language of enormous elasticity and emotional sensitivity; of quick hilarious banter and a welter of references both historical and mythological; it is an instrument of imaginative depth and scope, which has been tempered by the community for generations until it can pick up and sing out every hint of emotional modulation that can occur between people. Many international scholars rhapsodize that this speech of ragged peasants seems always on the point of bursting into poetry."

Further on she picks up the theme on a deeper level. "The way so-called depth psychologists go on about the subconscious nowadays you'd swear they had invented it, or at the very least stumbled on to a ghostly and ghastly continent whence mankind had previously never set foot. Even the dogs in the street in West Kerry know that the "otherworld" exists, and that to be in and out of it constantly is the most natural thing in the world. The easy interaction with the imaginary means that you don't have to have a raving psychotic breakdown to enter the "otherworld." The deep sense in the language that something exists beyond the ego envelope is pleasant and reassuring, but it is also a great source of linguistic and imaginative playfulness, even on the most ordinary and banal of occasions."

Lewis Thomas was right when he commented in the final pages of *Lives of A Cell* that perhaps our central purpose as human beings is to ferry language and its myriad manifestations into the future. We are all bees in the honeyed hive of language.

The diversity of languages, like the diversity of species, is founded in landscapes; mountains, rivers, seas and deserts impound and amplify our various linguistic streams. After the collapse of imperial Rome, the Pyrenees and Alps isolated Latin speakers into provincial dialects that evolved into Spanish, French and Italian. The ethno-linguistic puzzle of Aboriginal California is nearly synchronous with the larger features of Californian geography. Long residency in a locale, dwelling in its *focus,* works resonance into language; local vernacular, the precious "mettle" of neighborhoods, is coined in the slow alchemy of humans rooted in place.

Focus—Latin for *hearth* ("the dwelling place of the household gods").

The deep wisdom and prescient witness of languages rooted and nourished in landscape seem archaic to modernity and its current shibboleth, the sharp-toothed "wisdom" of the market. It is telling that the defining metaphor of recent society, "the bottom line", derives from a business profit and loss statement. Evidently our reality is founded on currency, cash flow and liquidity. No wonder our endeavors seem to float and drift rather than root or stand. Money and the easy logic of profit have conspired with hyper-inventive technologies to foster a civilization addicted to speed and change, revolution rather than evolution. The fossil-fueled mechanics and spendthrift energetics of modern civilization and its entropic friction with the natural world have serious consequences for the conservative dynamics of language. Market-induced entropy has overwhelmed and obliterated indigenous dialects, witness the Amazon, and demeans our present speech into a creature of advertisement rather than eloquence. But business and the market are not identical. The market is a mercurial roil of appetite, ambition and opportunity. Business and labor are the boat and crew that ride its weather. The heart of the market is profit, but the traditional heart of business is trade, relationship. Business crafts and trades often speak vividly of their endeavors. Investment originally meant to clothe.

Certainly language is not static. Words are born and die; like other life forms they adapt their behaviors to fit new circumstances, new weather. Words may spiral through a classical, almost formal, transformation from an original meaning to its opposite. The pilgrimage takes around three hundred years. C.S. Lewis in *Studies in Words*, followed the word *sad* through its peregrinations, documenting its turns with wry insight and wit.

In Chaucer's time *sad* meant full, the way you feel after a large meal, drowsy on the couch after Christmas dinner. *Sad* as full, can—by a small metaphoric stretch...also mean heavy. So it wasn't long before *sad* implied weight, heft. Further on in its gyre *sad* as weighty or full became *sad* as solid, firm, sound; "heavy" as we said in the sixties. Then *sad* as solid came to describe human character. A man or woman of solid character was *sad*. *Sad* applied to persons of dignity and quality; elders, tested and tempered were full *sad*. But character can age into gravity and severity and it's not far from the grave and serious sense of *sad* to our present sense of *sad* as tristesse or melancholy. *Sad's* pilgrimage reflects our changing perception of the elderly but its journey is also revealing because although *sad* shifted its attention as it traveled through time, it never lost its root sense of fullness (sated!) The bloom of the word changed color and shape in the slow roll of human weather but its roots were firm. *Sad's* journey happened in what we might call natural time, an evolution confirmed by small changes. But times have changed. For the last 150 -200 years English has switched its "watch" from natural time to commercial time. Natural time is grounded in cycles, the blooms, tides and seasons of human beings on the earth. In the quicksilver reality of global markets and modern technics, landscape is irrelevant. In money's abstract reality the map is the territory! I remember talking with a corporate forester who sadly remarked that accountants who couldn't tell a hemlock from a Douglas fir now managed timber harvest.

Words fare no better than souls or small birds in the reductive heat of commercial-industrial time. Consider the word *bad*. *Bad* has recently somersaulted through our speech, its gyre a circus act rather than a stately shadowy round dance, a revolution rather than an evolution. When I was a child in the late forties and early fifties, *bad* meant wicked, a sense still close to its root meaning of "open to all influence especially the worst." By the time I was in high school, *bad* still meant wicked to my parents but to my peers and me it meant brazen, tough, strong and fearsome. By the seventies, Michael Jackson had promoted *bad* into a term that evoked daring and personal power. *Bad* nearly finished its loop in thirty years. I fear for *bad;* we may have exhausted it, fried it in the overheated rush of our impotent ennui-driven need for clever new twists of speech to advertise our "attitude."

In the turbulent flux of our diversions, words are disappearing as fast as Amazonian song birds in a clear-cut, not to mention the degrading effects

51

of recent commercial efforts to mine the language resource to produce new hybrid words, word alloys to smooth the skid road of commerce. Think of the car names or the titles of perfumes or the pop monikers of breakfast cereals and toilet paper; Accura, Obsession, Turbo, Kix, Downy, soulless words, unredeemed vacant-eyed hustles, toxic schemes swept along in the fertile river of our gab. The artificial hybridization and kidnaping of words by commercial hype tends to thin and poison the character of our speech; slang on the other hand tends to renew it. I regret that there is not room in this essay to delve into the yeasty role slang and the jagged edge of underworld vernaculars play in "rapping," inflecting, inspecting, infecting and deflecting the pretensions of mainstream culture. The underworld with its pimps, carnies, shills, bums, burlesques, whores, crooks, tramps, junkies, punks and sharks; with its smothered ethnicity and twisted ambition, has been fertilizing English since its quickening with the Norman arrow in good King Harold's eye. Slang lives in the shadows of conventional speech, inventive, quick, predatory, afraid, feared, ignored and hence subversive. Slang mocks our conventions and by its bravado helps the language turn. Imagine a sinister half-starved jester whispering into the fat right ear of the sleeping king, napping on a Lear jet bound for tomorrow.

Notwithstanding the underworld's best efforts, students of English report that English is losing its spoken vocabulary, the diversity of its *terms,* despite its eminence as the lingua franca of the planet. And therein lies the reason for its malaise. Perhaps English is forfeiting its descriptive power because it has assumed a generic monocultural perspective. Still, there remain spirited English vernaculars, dialects of local color and weather-quickened wit. (I recall my West Texas brother-in-law's description of Ross Perot as a hand grenade with a bad haircut.) But the neighborhoods of these loric idioms are increasingly vulnerable to the acetone commercial media and its "solvent" capacity to smudge the subtlest and brightest hues of lingo. It is difficult indeed for indigenous beings: birds, words, plants, critters and perhaps now even weather to escape the money driven institutionalized revolution embodied in modern growth capitalism. But permanent revolution—cultural, economic or political—is terror as real as Robespierre's, Stalin's, Khomeni's or Mao's. We are conspiring with that terror in the way we've let ourselves be named. We are now by consensus and our own calling, consumers. The word consumer derives from a Latin word *consumo* ("to spend everything, to destroy utterly, to destroy by fire").

Market **from Latin** *merc* **("merchandise"), hence ("commerce, mercy [the price of pity?]") and ("Mercury, god of trade, speedy messenger") and ("secret thief") and lastly ("guide to souls to the otherworld").**

In a kind of delusional apologetics we now equate consumption with citizenship. But as late as eighty years ago *consumer* had negative connotations. We used the term to name a selfish and wanton sort. The change in the word's usage testifies to a changed society. Eighty years ago we called ourselves neighbors, citizens, and brothers and sisters, kith and kin. Neighbor is an Old English word which meant near fellow dweller. Citizen is from an Indo-European root *ci* or *cei* (" to lie down, to rest"), the same root gives us ("home") and cemetery"); a citizen is a homebody, a deep dreamer. *Kith and kin* arrives via Old English *cyth* ("native land"), and *cynn* ("kindred, one's own kind"), hence *kith and kin* ("the local haunt").

Like any living creature English wants to know where it is; where we have ferried it now...it isn't Sherwood Forest. Now spoken English surely lives with commerce having become estranged from local culture and the places that engender it.

> *Culture* from Latin *colere* ("to turn, to till the earth"). The poetry in "culture" is implicit. The soil is the past, the ancestors. Practicing culture we turn the ancestors into the light so they may bloom and nourish us. Culture is soil born.

English presently has more words in its spoken vocabulary for money than it does for moving water: bread, bucks, dough, change, cash, whip-out (my favorite), long green, swag, roll, stash, dibs, currency, quid, pile, jingle, lucre, pelf and plastic are only the skim of a longer list that doesn't include technical terms for money and monetary transactions. These words describe specific and nuanced relations to money; whip-out is not a term favored by investment bankers, nor is pelf or lucre likely to leap into the hipster's rap. English is faithfully articulating our reality, firming and confirming the current edge between us and the larger world. The rub is that our world by the witness of our words is becoming a fantasy, the placeless, neighborless realm of modern commerce.

In contrast consider these words, that name places and things that unspoken may be unnoticed: *lea* ("a meadow drenched in sunlight"); *rill* (" a small forceful stream"); *lynn* (" a pool beneath a waterfall"); *beck* (" a small brook") and *brook* (" a break-out in the bank of a larger stream that waters a marsh") and lastly *kelt* (" a spawned-out salmon or hung-over reveler. Speaking these words may re-articulate and re-enliven our world. The Northwest poet William Stafford said, "Sometimes a poem is writ to let one word breathe." The true genius of English, its poetic eye and musical ear, the subtle temper of its humor, is reticent, musing in the hinterlands "out of touch," waiting out the scourge of money's reductive fire, faithfully naming and calling the winds, rains, and creatures of the neighborhood, the kith and kin of the natural world forsaken by its mother tongue.

In the early sixties two bioregional visionaries, Freeman House and Jeremiah Gorsline, used Peter Berg's term "reinhabitation" to describe a social antidote to the devastation of natural and human communities by economies of transient consumerism. They proposed that the most revolutionary act was to settle permanently in a place and assume responsibility for the neighborhood with all the near fellow dwellers, mountains, rivers, flora and fauna and, I might add, English. We must reinhabit our language as well as our ecologies. If we stay put in deed and word our selfish rap will gradually unravel and in time re-weave us deeper into place; our speech will become part of the texture of locality, its felt meaning. Then our reality might once again resound with ancestral echoes and the myriad voices of the weather and the land. Our words will become again the welcome and the witness of our home's peculiar beauty and our lore will last nurtured in the practiced cycles of locality.

Imagine your home-place: the giant oak in the park, the bandstand with the leaky roof, the white ice-scoured mountains, the evergreen forests and thigh -thick winter steelhead, the polished stone of your father's grave. Imagine the familiar surround and the horizon of words that holds your world as the rim of a bell. Imagine you are the tongue of that bell, silent and still in its shelter. The tongue cannot will itself to move and ring the bell, only the swollen wave of weather's mystery may move tongue and bell together and ring out familiar music.

*Nuala Ni Dhomhnaill in the *New York Times Book Review.*

There Is No Art for Art's Sake:
The Blossoms Are Ghosts at the Wedding

FORTY YEARS AGO I WITNESSED the casting of bronze sculpture. Perhaps it was the Vulcanic river of metal or the fragile bone white molds, but the pour converted me and I began a lifetime relationship with art and artists. Bronze casting for sculptors has been a fruitful and educational association. Each new work requires detailed physical consideration of the piece, its nature and how best to translate it into metal. These considerations are usually practical, dealing with the material, logistic and structural aspects of translation of images from one material to another. There is always some private or shared reflection on the nature of the piece: what it wants to be. Philosophical musings are not foremost in my work but they do haunt, enliven, curse and bless it. I realize that although I know when a *piece* is "art," I can't always explain my perception. Perhaps it is because art has become an all inclusive and hence blurry term. It no longer deepens our experience or vitalizes our understanding. We only vaguely know what we mean when we say art. Few dare ask, "What is art?"

The word *art* sprouts from the Indo-European root word *ar* or *er* (" to fit together"). The root generates words to describe joints, joinery and joining of all kinds. *Art's* verbal family includes arm (the related limb?), article, articulate, armature, and *inert* ("ill fitted, ill-jointed, unable to move"); *inert* is *art's* opposite, ("inart"). Other cognates are arithmetic, arthritis, ratio, reason, read, ritual and harmony. All these words are haunted and enlivened by the root notion, *ar* (" fitted together"). Ritual is a fit with the gods. Reason is fitting things or ideas together. Ratio is a mathematical description of fit. Harmony is the tone of a fit. *Artus* in Latin was also the male member, the joint. Art *is* seminal, the fit is lively.

Art is a fitting together, a well-made joint, an articula*tion,* the way the bones in your fingers work together, or words in a Yeats' poem, or an osprey's wings in a light wind. Art is a primal and ancient form of connection. The first art object may have been "discovered" by a *homo habilis* person 400,000 years ago. This ancestor of *homo sapiens* who had fire and probably language found a hand-sized, round stone that appeared to have eyes. Was the stone "looking" or "seeing", who knows? We do know that the eyes were not made by human hands; they were naturally occurring depressions in the "face" of the stone. We also know that the stone was an object of veneration because it was purposely stained with red ochre to mark it as sacred, to acknowledge special connection with "the stone with eyes".

Before the superficial, speed-fed blur of modern media, art traditionally articulated our world, weaving imagination into local context, knotting the treads of our experience into meaning, re-presenting it in sacred light. In shrines, songs, dances, bells, drama and lore, it cadenced our mortal vitality, shadowing it with beauty. Art's joining and jointing is not mechanical or reductive. Art is not a circus contraption. It is an invitation to belong to creation, to share and acknowledge its endeavor. It is crafting the fit of inspiration and material that is the creative act. Inspiration and material are gifts and art doesn't belong to the artist, he belongs to it.

Art's joinery, its "fitting together" is *metaphoric* from Greek *meta* ("beyond") and *pherein* ("to carry, to bear"), hence, our metaphor "to carry beyond,"— imagination and practiced perception rowing the boar of surprise. Art is metaphoric craft that ferries us beyond ourselves. The inspired artist transforms his medium into a nexus, a crossroads of material and mystery, a landmark of wonder, a well to quench our thirst, a focused stillness, an oddly familiar room to attend the whisper behind the curtained door. Art is a way-point in life's stumbling bruise of amazement, the evening path in the forest, an intimate human-trod edge with un-knowing "familiar mystery." The artist mid-wifes our way into the startling weather of the secret world. Art's "articulations" encourage us, give us heart to listen to the other, to welcome the guest who shows the way.

We should remember that, while etymologies deepen our sense of art's "work," they may also demean art's larger mission of transformation and communication. If we were to curse it with an exclusive etymological ball and chain, we reduce it to clever joinery. Art's works, its articulations, are often paradoxical and chimeric, even magical, revealing by concealing, a silk cloak thrown on a fickle breeze. Art is not merely telling, it is also the alchemical coaxing of matter's shy soul into clear witness. Art is not a trick; it is a trickle, a spring of unknown source that quenches our thirst and the cup that lets you drink.

Traditionally the artist's work pivoted on, and was informed by, his materials. They located and centered his inspiration. The material was the *medium,* the body that let the ghost of his inspiration live. Our word material derives from a Latin word *materia* ("timber, wood"), and by extension, other materials, "stuff" we use. *Materia* came from the Latin word *mater* ("the hard part of a tree, the trunk that produced shoots"). This *mater* is a transferred use of *mater* ("mother"). *Mater* comes from the Indo-European root *ma* ("breast"). *Mater* is the "nourisher." When you cut down *mater* you get *materia*, hence, our *material* ("the dead mother"). In pre-Christian Europe the great mother goddess was all-powerful and ubiquitous. Her milk ran in streams and issued forth in springs. Rhea was the mother of the gods; her name meant to flow.

Maybe artists and their intimacy with "materials" are secretly coaxing Rhea's bounty, inviting it to well up through our simple monuments and quench the fire-parched thirst of the fathers. Art is digging for water with a word. There is no art for art's sake; the blossoms are ghosts at the wedding. No wonder we knock on wood for luck.

LAND, EARTH, SOIL, DIRT:

SOME NOTES TOWARDS A SENSE OF PLACE

YEARS AGO, THE MORNING AFTER an evening of beer drinking and poetry reciting, a hung over clot of revelers were walking back from breakfast. Northwest poet Robert Sund, whom I had met the night before, lagged behind the rest of us, preoccupied. He had stopped and was staring into a corner, a crack where two concrete buildings met. Curious, we went back; he looked up from a small cranial-shaped pile of moss and said something like, "That's our only hope." We laughed nervously, a little shaken, it struck us all. The moss was patiently turning the buildings to soil, to dirt, to earth. That moment has haunted me since, and the *idea* of soil and its import has become a recurrent meditation for me.

I want to look at soil as a metaphor, as a self-darkened lens that bends light, dividing, revealing, obscuring; a lens to watch light thickened green by life and kneaded rich by death's dark hands. I want to behold a rainbow as the faint echo of soil's gravid hive. Imagine soil as the *context,* the textural background of other imaginations, an other darker nature grounding culture, personality, language. A good place to start is in the words we use about soil. By examining, exhuming the stories hidden in them, we reveal a strata of unconscious attitudes towards soil. We say "back to the land," "mother earth," "good ground," "dirty," but only vaguely know what we're saying. Our descriptions lack discrimination, want felt meaning. Reviewing the stories biding in the words and following their instruction, we may resuscitate a poetic, a way of seeing and knowing the local world we walk upon.

Land is a word nearly synonymous with soil. We cultivate, plow and till the land. But these are activities originally germane to soil. Their use with land is an example of the natural poetic license that dwells in language. Land is from the Indo-European root *lendh* ("open land"). This sense still adheres to the cognates of *lendh.* Old English has *land* meaning specifically ("open land"). French has *lande* ("heath, moorland, especially infertile moorland"). Our word lawn comes to us from French *lande.* Old Slavic has *ledo* ("wasteland").

German has additionally *landau* ("water meadow") (land + *owa* [water]). Old Celtic has *landa* ("a valley"). Welsh and Cornish have *lann* ("an enclosure"). *Land* is a relatively abstract term that refers to boundaries. Its basic idea is open or closed space. Its root does not refer to any other specific aspect of landscape except its openness or closedness. At heart, it's about "land shape," about surface, not soil.

Land's meaning for us is *owned topography*. The idea of property is the word's current context. To express other qualities of landscape requires qualification: heart land, forest land. Land no longer constellates an image. We can "land" anywhere. There is a land romance: some of us went "back to the land." But it is telling that we went back to the land (an abstraction) not to the Palouse, the Olympic Rain Forest, or even the heath, desert or forest. Part of the difficulty of the back-to-the-land movement is that its speech does not adequately inform its impulse. For us land is a concept, not a locality.

Earth is another word we substitute for *soil*. It is a word with a surprising spectrum of meanings. Its root is the Indo-European *er* ("earth, anciently and essentially the place between the heavens and the land of the dead"). It is the name of our planet, earth, gravity's burrow, the invisible genius that keeps our feet on the ground and tethers moons swole scythe-like magic. Gravity, whose pull prescribes and consecrates our orbit and allows our blue-green fire-hearted dream to dance its tragic dance around a dying star.

We cannot yet "buy earth"—we find that hard to say. Historically, earth has meant or still means: the world, cosmos, soil, surface, country, chemical oxide, the place between heaven and hell, electrical ground (British), a grave, a burrow, a shelter. To condense all these meanings we might say earth is the place of fundamental, fateful connection.

Dirt is the unsavory side of our descriptions of soil. *Dirt* is from Old Norse *drit* ("excrement"). *Drit* is from Old Norse *drita* ("to shit"). It is telling that we use a word with that root to describe soil. Healthy soil digests shit and puts it to use, but dirt and soil are not the same. Granted, soil can be dangerous if fouled by poisons or diseased wastes, but we are missing the fundamental difference between soil and dirt when we confuse them. Soil is a "community enterprise." Shit is potential nutrients "looking for work." We do *dirt* dirty, using it as a synonym for soil or earth. We should maintain its specific connections to excrement. Earth and soil are not shit. An earthy mind and dirty mind are different gatherings. I wonder if there isn't a ruling class prejudice hiding in the continued confusion of dirt and soil. It's almost as if the soil were beneath us instead of holding us up.

Ground is another word associated with soil. Ground is from Old English *grund* ("foundation, earth"). *Ground* means bottom; a "groundling" was originally a name for a fish that lived on the bottom of ponds or a person who preferred, or could only afford, the pit in front of the stage. *Ground* means fundamental, basic. We run aground; we are well-grounded in thought. Many disciplines use the word (carpentry, naval terminology, philosophy, engineering, art, etc.). Ground is cognate with Old English *grynde* ("abyss"). So, *ground* is cousin to *depth* and *mystery*. It is also used in reference to soil and landscape. We work the ground, the groin (also from *grynde* ("abyss") of the earth. Perhaps we confuse soil and ground because soil grounds us, soil is *fundamental;* it *grounds* us. It completes the circuit.

Finally we come to soil, "the root metaphor," "our only hope." Soil is the secret sublimation of the land. It is the black, alchemic gold of this green earth, the re-enchantment of waste and death. It is the humming dignity of the gravid ground, the black honey of our sun-drenched hive. Soil is an earthy, grounding term that is not land. Soil is not easily owned or domesticated. It suffers our earthly antics with motherly patience calmly awaiting our return. Soil's history as a term is fascinating. In time it has meant: a wild boar mire, a pool of water used as a refuge by hunted deer, sexual intercourse, composition of the ground, mold, staining, to purge a horse on green feed.

Etymologically, soil has two roots. First, soil is from Indo-European *su* ("to produce young"). Cognate words are sow, succulent, socket, hyena and hog. Pigs were sacred to the earth goddess. Pigs and snakes were her favored images. The sense that comes to us from this root is mire or stain, but behind these senses—"in the roots wild pigs are breeding and birthing at the mired edge of ancient oak forests; deer are dying near a hidden pool." "Soiled" we touch the sacred suckling succulent sow.

Soil's other sense (ground-earth) comes to us from Latin *solum* ("ground floor, threshing floor") and the obsolete ("solium, throne"). The Indo-European root is *sed* (" to sit, to settle"). Soil's cognates are nest, nestle, seat, soot, cathedral, sole. Soil is where we stand. The "soles" of our feet touch the soil, grounding us. "He's got his feet on the ground." Soil is a throne of bones where light nests, where we settle. The ancestors tickle our feet from its fertile shade.

Soil is a kind of bicameral word. Like a good two-house legislature, it "converses." The two root meanings, *fertility* and *seat*, have intertwined since Middle French, when the words became identical in sound and spelling. Indeed the sow is enthroned in soil. Soil is the throne, the nest that bears young, the queen' s room. Soil is the land in hand, smelled and seen. Soil supports the living and receives the dead.

The science of ecology affirms the etymological complexity of soil. From *Ecology and Field Biology* by Robert Leo Smith: "Soil is the site where nutrient elements are brought into biological circulation by mineral weathering. It also harbors the bacteria that incorporate atmospheric nitrogen into the soil. Roots occupy a considerable portion of the soil. They serve to tie the vegetation to the soil and to pump water and its dissolved minerals to other parts of the plant for photosynthesis and other biochemical processes—vegetation in turn influences soil development, its chemical and physical properties and organic matter content. *Thus soil acts* as *a 'sort of pathway' between the organic and mineral worlds.*

In short, soil is the bridge between the living and the dead, both in one, a living death, a paradox. Geologist Robert Curry explains the crucial connection between soil and human life: "All (forms of) life, without exception, are dependent upon out-side sources of nutrients for their support within a substrate upon which they nurture themselves. In all non-marine systems, the ultimate substrate is soil. Even marine systems are dependent upon weathered minerals derived by soil-forming processes throughout geologic time on land. Soil is not an inert inorganic blanket of varying thickness on the land that can be differentiated into subsoil and topsoil. Those naive terms belie a basic misunderstanding that permeates the agricultural advisory services of this country. Soil is generally recognized by soil scientists to be a dynamic, living assemblage of precisely bio-geochemically segregated macro- and micro-nutrient ions held in a series of remarkable storage sites. These nutrients are provided by slow weathering over geologic time and are translocated and reprocessed by soil organisms and plant activity. In general the living biomass beneath the ground equals or exceeds that above ground.[!]

Soil is thus not a mineral, geologic resource but a biospheric resource that, although renewable, can reform only at extremely slow geologic rates of tens of centuries. The soil nutrients within their delicately segregated geo-chemical levels represent precisely and literally the sum total of the long sustainable economic capital of the nation."

To paraphrase Curry, we might say soil is fate. This notion resonates with soil's connections to seats of power, the sow goddess, soil our destiny, our destination. Soil is the land in hand, a specific place. Soil embodies the meeting, is the meat of weather and rock; "remembers" them into trees and kingfishers, salamanders and salal. Each location knots that meeting differently. Your county soil survey becomes a kind of earth phrenology—soil is a live being, a dark leaf breathing water and light. Soil is myriad neural serpents writhing knotted on an infinity of their discarded skins. It is its own renewable research, a porcine cannibal lover, phoenix, shit-eating alchemist, Ouroboros enshrined, an honest mother. Persephone, Goddess of spring lives underground, ensoiled. She rises in spring, wife of wise Hades, King of Wealth and Death. Her name means "bringer of destruction." Perhaps she is a personification of soil, the living death. Demeter's virginal daughter married to the king of the dead. (Interestingly, in one of his myriad seductions, Zeus, the king of heaven, approached Persephone in the guise of a snake as she sat in the great cave of creation weaving the threads of destiny.) Plants and animals follow her back into the light. Soil blurs the distinction between the living and the dead, humbling us. Soil is the pious Confucian son tending the graves of the ancestors. It is husband and wife in one dark body. Soil is the dwelling wave, the archetypal, renewable resource. *Resource* from *re-surge* ("to surge back"), and *surge* is from Latin *sub-regere* ("to rule from below"). So, a resource surges back ruled by powers hidden from view. Soil is the paradoxical death-dark well of our living. Soil is the resurrecting, hidden ruler, fatemaker, dark-eyed, blossom-giddy girl weaving destiny deep in the ground.

We are all earth-born, literally and figuratively, and the word human confirms this assertion. Our words human, humble and homage all derive from Latin *humus* ("earth, soil, ground, region, country"). A human is earth-born, shares the quality of humus. It is well to remember that to our ancestors humus was local and that "humanity" was born, arose from a specific locale, a place. The people over the hill might not be quite human, in the sense of your local humus. Our language knows we are earth-born even if we think we are heaven sent.

Human awareness is the blossom in the fertile mix of two soils, the soil of language and the soil of place. The "soil" of language is not merely metaphoric, it is mortally real. Language wants a place, a locus, as much as you or I. Vernaculars are living proof of languages rooting and blooming where it lands. Language grows into where it lives, symbiotic; old world metaphors re-sown into new landscapes. Our perceptions and our witness catch the stark light and green it into meaning. These meanings compost and compose a deeper experience of where we are. Words are living beings; they borrow our breath for inspiration; they blossom, fruit, root and die.

Language in place, ensoiled, inevitably blooms culture. Culture in root means to plow, return, cycle. Understood etymologically, culture is soil homage. Culture grows out of and dies back into language in place; the stories enrich the words. Culture is the sacred blossom; it consecrates the ground, soul and soil of the same dark being.

Western society has abandoned the older notion of culture, the husbanding of human life in place. Our culture does not arrive through the discrimination of the different songs the wind rings in the several pines of the Sierras, or the terror of the child lost in the rain forest, or the shape of a fisherman's pipe; no, instead we buy our culture. It is a consumer item, an *uncouth* import.

Whether it was dire necessity or some fatal species-specific flaw we took to the wind with a cross and sword. We learned to grow anywhere, choke out the natives. (Aboriginal often peoples die of homesickness.) We came to favor shallow roots, learned to grow in places we wasted. This may be what we really are, but our language once lived in a neighborhood where the word for tree and truth were the same—Indo-European *dru*, whence ("truth, tree, trust, druid"), etc. Each speech has an accent, the odor of composted history. If left alone, our patterns of speech become localized, "dried" by the heat, made pungent by rain. But our electric neighborhood ignores locality; dialogue is now electrified. Blind as a volt, our tongues are in the radared air, groundless. TV is our tree.

The soil is where we return our dead; it is the home of the ancestors. This sense of soil is lacking for most of us. We are careless. I have not witnessed the lives and deaths of my kin. True to the American dream, we scattered, seeking private versions of wealth, ignoring Hades' dark treasure. I am less for my lack of witness. Human life grows in weight and intensity as people stay in one place. The ancestors form a wedge behind us, press us forward on the edge of that weight. Depending on our ability to bear the weight, to balance it, our located word is good and drives deeper into the haunt of home or it breaks and we float up into the vapid torrent of commercial culture. Without the ancestors, without the soil of souls, we are potted plants, doomed in real weather. When we speak of living here, we should remember that perhaps the most important thing we will do here is die here, that our deaths will matter and be the first step in steadying our children's steps. Our graves will anchor them while they work the subtle weather of this cedar-green world. Soil supports the living and receives the dead.

Tilth
Tilth comes from Old English *tilian* ("to work hard for, to cultivate"), with associated words in Dutch, Celtic and German that mean opportunity, agreeable and pleasant. To till is to work hard, to strive for the good and agreeable. Tilth, then, is the quality of carefully tended and worked soil, a term that belongs to the farm and ancient soil of our speech. If we stay put long enough we might some day say of a good story teller, "Her words have tilth."

Culture Is a Mortal Nest

WALKING THE FOREST PATH IN WINTER, the few bare trees and brush in this evergreen world bloom again in empty nests: wren nests, robin nests, nests once secret bowers in summer's verdant haze now stark dun gray blossoms, cupped skyward in the dark bony arms of trees bereft of green and sleeping now in its absence.

In the elderberry and alder thicket, a shadow of a patch we cut for cedar house-poles; I spot a wren's nest, hoary with moss, its spiny twigs weak with rot. This woven bowl with bits of blue egg, the subtle variety of its weft, fragrant and savory in the winter snap, holds me in an hallucination of scale. I imagine the lip of the nest as a ridge in the landscape and closing my eyes I peer into a mountain swale, dark forest and chimney smoke feint and fey in the air; I expect to hear singing but none arrives. This begged shape, this sewn bowl, this nest fascinates and stirs an older soul in me that unbidden *reads* the runes in old clothes, the hand haunting the discarded glove, the coursing stream beneath the city street.

This mortal nest perched starkly in the leafless thicket, the wren's spring-green secret recalls the biblical statement, "The birds and the beasts have their lairs but the son of man has no home." And my mordant muse returns to question, "Where is your home? Where is the grave wherein your ghost might dwell?" And I drift into the confusion that dogs my modern days, confusion of the illiterate guest in this fateful forest, alive in a language as strange as I am to the soul of this place. This reverie refracts into my unease with modern life, contemporary culture, this electric neon nest, haunted by an imagination that is a manic hybrid of demonic mercantile wit and mechanical skill, a sexy automaton that titillates but cannot breed or die and is learning to clone itself, the mirage in the mirror polished by the smooth abrasion of money—money, solvent of soul, precipitous, volatile, any value cashed in and wagered. The ancient essential masks of the world become kindling for money's fiery hunger.

And before me this mortal nest, this cupped silence and its bits of sky-speck-led eggs, deepens the reverie, reminds me culture is a mortal nest, a woven circle nestled in the trees, founded in the dark, wind-deft accuracy of intu-ition, our various breaths weft and waft among the fir's vernacular. The nest is a place the soulful birds find and found; the quick darting intelligence of wren, the aural patient wit of robin, plaiting their nests in the right places, in nooks, crooks, elbows, sills, hollows, ledges and edges, small cogent syn-chronies sustained over and over; the nest rebuilt and repaired, haunting the deep-rooted, light-loving truthful tree. *Culture is a mortal nest;* this phrase affirms the natural association of birds and souls: "A little bird told me," the falling priapic bird-headed man and his avian staff painted so delicately on the walls of Lascaux.

The nest is a circle, a prescience of eternity assembled locally, moss, twigs, bark, string, leaves, bits of this and that, a poetic vernacular, an architecture of renewal articulated in the poignant beauty of necessity. Likewise, culture is the human cycle artfully fitted to locality, articulated into the "biologic" and "ecologic" of the place, harmonious and resonant with the ecology, the legend of the house (*oikos, eco-*). Contrast this nest notion of culture with the conventional wisdom that culture is an entertainment, a diversion; it's aim, distraction not enchantment and transformation—the seminal discipline of a death song.

Culture is a mortal nest, its shape central to the cycle of dwelling. The nest is built by male and female to shelter and raise up their young. The nest is the inevitable shape of dwelling and yet the young must leave it to try the form again, renewing the nest in the neighborhood. And always the wild card: the young raven flies north, the salmon turns up the "wrong" creek; new worlds to try the old form. The young find courage and heart in the nest and its obligatory arrangement. Still many nests fail and become threads in a larger nest, a (revolving, evolving) synchrony wherein the living remain to re-artic-ulate the ancestor's haunt. *Culture is a mortal nest;* this sodden nest before me about to fall in December rain. The nest eventually feeds the tree as the tree shelters the nest, all beings articulating the ever-darkening, mysterious light into smaller and smaller nests, secret rooms where old women with egg-tooth haberdashery dance in silence, dark pools where blind trout flash....

Culture is a mortal nest. The nest must be worked and reworked in place. Curiously the etymology of *culture* traces its roots to Latin *colere, cultus* ("to turn and re-turn the soil"). (Soil is also a mortal nest, cultivation turns its fertile past into quickening present light.) The metaphoric heart of culture is not abstract, it belongs to the plutonic wealth of the soil under ground; it belongs to places, the little world, the *herba buena* and wild strawberries

66

on the sunny hillside. In the human world it is the alchemical composting of moments, taking the food value out of history, growing myth in the dark soil of the past.

Culture is the tempo and shape of the human fit with local nature. It is the human complement to weather, our gift to the larger world. The forms of culture are changed and worked as the form of a boat is worked by generations to fit the local waters, hence local *craft:* dories, canoes, coracles, punts, rafts, kayaks, outriggers and skiffs, etc., hence poems, jokes, folktales, superstitions, carols, chants, song and keens. Culture is worked not invented. You can't invent soil. It is the way a cherished song, polished by use, bears the daily life of people, not noisy ivory tower heroics. The diverse forms of culture are not static as totalitarian governments propose, nor revolutionary as the entrepreneurs and the avant-garde maintain; rather they are conservative. Like a grandmother's reveries, lively, ribald and deeply wise, culture's stories and songs bear us on in time evolving, rolling slowly forward, not running in fashionable circles; a narrative changes by inspiration and necessity into nuanced connections to the neighborhood, mythos, a language that names the many hands of rain or the color of cedar trees at dusk.

Culture is a mortal nest, a temporary home in the trees, our children's bed, our burden; the firm ledge they leap from, their precipice, the barrow of our love. *Culture is a mortal nest;* Curiously, nest is related etymologically to silence and situate. They share a common root *si.* So there is an original connection between silence, situation and nesting. Perhaps it is because there is a fundamental silence in every situation, every nest. Maybe true culture seeks to grace that silence, congratulate it, like prayer or dancing at a wake or a wedding.

Culture rises from silence as plants rise from the soil; each human being a kind of seed or larva that may or may not hatch in the silent light-darkened soil. Culture nests in silence; broods in silence, silence is its secret fertility, its mystery, the weather and light its beckoning consort.

Culture is a mortal nest, your grandmother's Sunday hat blown off in a black Easter storm, stuck upside down in a ghost berry bush—waiting for the egg.

BEACON

THE FIRST TIME I SAW A WOMAN NAKED I was six years old and it was the spring of 1949 in St. George, Utah. The winter garden had been dug up and the beanpoles set in the dark red dirt. I was playing hide and seek with my cousin Wally and in the middle of our chase I called time out and flew into my grandmother's white clapboard house to pee. I burst into the bathroom without knocking and there was grandma Jen, just stepped out of the shower.

Her gray-streaked auburn hair was loose and down to her waist. She had a shower cap in her hand and was reaching for a towel. Time stopped for me. Her face, neck and arms were a ruddy tan from years spent hiking in the high desert sun. But her nakedness was a creamy, lightly freckled plump robustness. She was a big-boned Scots woman who could work with the men. But it was her breasts that held me in stunned fascination, beckoning me not in an overtly sexual way but an awakening, fateful way, the mysterious invitation and promise of otherness. She was at that moment its emissary. Every man knows, though few admit, that women are the crucible of our character; that a woman traditionally frames and invites a man's fate. Grandma Jen was a bounteous Venus who, for a few stunned seconds, revealed a mystery that still beckons. Then she spoke in a calm and dignified voice while she reached unpanicked for a large towel, "Tom, you'll have to wait outside while I dry off and dress. I'll be out in a few minutes." Her voice brought me to my senses and I suddenly felt dizzy from the scent of lavender soap and stumbled out the door.

Later that visit grandma Jen took me hiking to the top of a mountainous white rock the locals called Sugar Loaf. It was higher than I'd ever been before. She asked if I'd like to peer over the edge. I said yes in a kid's unknowing, slightly fearful way. She wisely took my hand and as we reached the edge vertigo, inspiration or madness, grabbed me and I stepped out into the deadly drop below the rock. Intuitively grandma Jen caught my fatal momentum on the first step and swung me in a quick arc over the void. We walked away from the edge and she said in a quiet reassuring way, "Let's creep up to the edge this time and see what we can see." We did and I don't know if she noticed or not because she was kneeling behind me and had her hand around my belt; but there 100 ft. down was a ledge and a dead fawn, two ravens pecking at its eyes. I didn't say anything and neither did she. My world changed forever.

THE LEAPER

THE DOCTOR WAS EXPLAINING how sperm moved, like salmon, and how the uterus gave them hold, created "current" so they knew which way to swim. I thought, "Jesus, salmon!" and I knew I was one once. It was as real as this: I could remember the slow torture of rotting still alive in a graveled mountain stream. Humped up, masked in red and green, dressed for dancing I was death's own delight, her hands caressing me…and this is the part I can't remember—whether she laughed or wept as we rolled in love.

3 • WIFE

The word *wife* is the green edge of an ancient word, *weip* or *weib* ("to tremble, to vibrate"). *Weip/weib* also animates ("wave, viper, whip, waiver"). In Old English *wif* meant ("woman, married woman"). In most archaic Germanic languages *wif* meant woman primarily and "wife" secondarily. Semantically the old Germanic words for woman (*wif, wib, weib, vif*) mean either "the vibrator" or "the veiled one." The veil vibrates in her world's mysterious wind; is she signaling or inviting?

Plainsong

Everyone is alone.
Fledglings left in the nest,
we even learn this alone.
Solitary we turn from dreaming
to the empty air around us…
in
to the plain girl in your heart
who is finally asked to dance.
She doesn't know that
you are death.
You would be kind;
dance well.

Klamath

Starless twilight
chicory blossom sky
crone's blind eye
focusing into darkness.

West wind haunts
the river valley
dry and leathery
as an aged Yurok widow's breasts.

Who is it
rustling live oak and madrone
with a fierce woman's touch
coaxing the summer fruit to earth?

We row hard
into this ancient prescient wind
on rafts pieced from parts
of a thousand nameless places
glad to have come this far together.

Masquer

Masquer,
you hide in me
like a snow owl
        in the wind.

Coasting in my own
          unsteady breeze
you hunt hidden and alone.

The Well

I dug my well in fall;
down through till and sand,
down in time
in blue till and clay
hunting a vein
ants and willows whispered over
all summer long.

I had my trusted tools,
strong simple magic,
an old truck axle
forged to break stone
and a rusted shovel
with a twice-busted handle.

A spade and a wand,
I held half a gypsy's hand
and I worried it with work
while I waited for the draw.

I chose a shape,
a path to follow down.
A circle this time,
last winter I dug
a square dry hole.
A circle for luck
and I dig it twisting into the earth
Coriolus even here…
The well spiraled down
miming the motion of its prey.

Down into the ground,
busting my body
in her hard gray flesh—
strange love of men
deep in the earth,
potent in mines,
in wells.

I worked on,
earth louse
hunting the blood
clouds buried there.
Last year's rain
crawled beneath me
in the stones,
cold thin wisdom whispering below me.

A slow spinning dancer,
mole patient,
I sank in the graveled dream
by the labor of my hands.
Down in time,
stepping through the fire
asleep in stone,
through red sparks
and the slow sulfured breath
of broken minerals.

Hunting a vein
I found treasures
buried eons.
Blind old stones
brought to light,
round crystalled rooms
opened accidentally;
and one day twenty feet down
a fist of black smoke
trapped in a ball of sand.

At night I dream of fountains,
baroque fantasies,
burbling angels of copper and lead;
and a black lake
buried ten thousand years
rising hungrily to greet
my forewarned feet.

I think of this well as a tattoo
on my grandmother's breast.
Think of it as a place
to store the songs of a drunken friend.
A well is as simple as this:
plain hard work,
you tap the earth;
break it open
and lift the pieces out.
Working down in earnest
you try to wake the water up.

Walking to the Barn

Walking to the barn
in the cold blue twilight
of this wintry day;
the water bucket steaming
to make warm mash for our toothless horse.
The horse is older;
the bucket heavier with the passing years.
We duck beneath the breeze-supple branches
of a young cedar seeking the
open light of the trail.
Its green brushes us as we pass,
Mall stops and whispers,
"To be touched by a tree is a blessing."

Beauty

Beauty is the world's gift
passed on in honest witness.

Cleverness may catch it
but stills its soul in clutching.

We stand on the edge
of a grave that wants a garden,
waiting for heart's old drum
to find a song.

There is no art
      for art's sake.

The blossoms are ghosts
      at the wedding

Eve

The red fruit refreshed Eve.
But the apple smoked in Adam's hand
like a coal.
And it was not her fine free care
he felt that day,
but some vague bearded fear
that made the sky go dry and cold;
a fear that poisoned clouds
and made Eve's smile grow old.

Elders

Salmon slap the work-scarred,
earth-curved decks of fish boats
like blind abandoned angels knocking
at a midnight door bereft…
The starry quicksilver glint of the sea
suffocating in our mortal air
and then
I've heard them slash the laughing rills
on moonless winter nights
dodging clawed phantoms
in the rock-creased stream.

But today watching
a water-bright bruise of dog salmon
brawl over this haunted gravel
for the first time in a decade…
I close my eyes and dream of
silver-skinned elders,
the old ones, spent and
weeping in welcome
for the clear-eyed rain.

Arrival

A moon-white moth
flutters easy as a magician's hand
in the candle-lit air…
searches the house
like the inside of his hat,
then disappears
just as you arrive.

Dru Oja Jay
born 2-23-80

Remains

We grow thin in time; our shadows stick.
The world presses our practiced skin
closer to our bones.
They wobble tree-slow almost stately
in our bodies' sea-soaked breeze.

Our well of tears surprises us;
we cry quietly at the funny parts of movies,
circus foolish in the approaching confusion.
No longer heroes we become
bewildered hobos in the screaming iron
boxcars of our remembering.

The tempered armor of our learning,
rusted stiff and thin
by our own strong weather,
is useless now. So we step out and
catch the fateful train
over the snow-white mountains of winter,
our tatter-veiled nakedness
the final witness
to the death-edged innocence
that remains.

Restoration

(for the Salmon Creek Crew—Cheri, Bob, Clif, Bruce, Noreen, Robbie)

When the ripened life of summer coils,
quickened like a press of darkling ghosts
in the ruddy luminosity of these eggs,
we begin to nurse their intent.

Bravely, as if we know their secret,
we attend these tender beings,
who are loyal only to the earth-sifted rain
and its sun-woven rivers.

Through flood, silt, disease
and the hungry shadows
of our pestilent civilization,
we have been faithful,
flirting on the edge of our common despair
with wonder.

Love

(for Sara Mall)

Love is not a flower.
A rose is the afterthought
        of love...
with its fragrance,
its thorns
and slowly fading colors

No, love is a root.
The water-split seed
drives deep into the ancient earth
to find strength to seek the day.
You are my drop of water
you are my darkest treasure
you are the honest sky.

4 • CLUE

Clue or *clew*—from Old English *cleowe, cleowen, cliwen, ball, skein.* These words are akin to claw, cloud, cleat, clod, and, perhaps, clown (originally a country bumpkin, a clodhopper). A ball of thread in ancient Greek myth and fact was used for finding one's way out of a labyrinth; hence a means of discovery, hence a discovery that assists in the solution of a crime or mystery. A clue is the end of an unraveled ball of thread, the beginning of an unraveled whole. We walk and wind, gathering our way into the light.

GEEZER

In the tentative sun of early April my son Dru and I hike out to Shi Shi, the poet's beach. In the sixties recluse poets and hippie visionaries built driftwood houses just out of wave reach in the shelter of wind-firm spruce. Navigating the muddy trail I muse on its dark mingle of life and death, of skunk cabbage, dead leaves and yesterday's rain…soil the color of Lauren Bacall's voice in a midnight room…dark mingle of body and mind rolling in the cloud-broken light and the blood-black trail and beyond my reverie the sea roars and smashes against the ancient lake-born stones of this coast.

Dru runs to the lucent waves as if they were old friends or a girl in a dream. His heart is his secret but his step is joyful in youth's unfettered praise for this marveled world.

At night the driftwood fire dies in misty rain. In the murmur of my son's gentle snore, my work-tempered bones settle like coastal mountains into the insistent sea of sleep. Barely awake I bob in its dark majesty like a wizened seal, "*geezer,*" I whisper to myself, "graybeard, guiser, masker, shape shifter," and recall the night that consecrated this late vocation, geezer, a whispered calling with no return address.

I was in the New York Tavern in Juneau, Alaska, wintertime. Brad Matsen and I were drinking frosted, lemon rinsed vodka, "lemon drops," to wash the weird melancholy of a book tour from our blood. We were watching a stately Tlingit Princess boogaloo in the middle of a churning crowd to a house band that had broken through to another realm. The princess, mantled in the spruce cool dignity of privilege seemed the bright flinty edge of an ancient story we could not hear. "Depart Reality!" was the zany refrain to our musings, and after seven straight lemon drops we walked without a wobble into the star-haunted night to witness the *Taku Winds,* a kind of cosmic nightcap. For Brad they were familiars, comrade killers, soul bracers, dangerous allies, the haunt and chorus of his youth as a Juneau troller. For me they were eerie and startling as meeting an old lover in the fog in Naples. The Taku Winds woke us up. They came willow-wa-ing, whipping the water, banshee-bright in the brisk blue starlight…howling forgotten ghosts of the dead, the land, ice and sea. Brad and I leaned into the stuttering gale as if we were in a rugby scrum with the ancestors! Laughing and hooting "Man, oh man," celebrating the dark, iridescent snake-whip ferocity of the blow, yet at the same time we were strangely still, "*kiting*," feet firm on the wharf, bodies nearly horizontal in the blast. Moth mad and stump-still we conspired with that most ancient air to glide between the stars and gravity, the invisible string on a geezer's mask, the glint in the graybeard's eye; buoyed up in the wind, coasting in the gravid undertow of this blessed, wounded world.

Note: *Geezer* ("old person") probably from obsolete *guiser* ("an actor") (see *guise*) but perhaps introduced by sailors and soldiers from Malta, via *gisem* ("the human body"), hence ("man") according to *Origins: A Short Etymological Dictionary of Modern English* by Eric Partridge. I like *guiser* as the root of geezer. *Guiser* comes from Old English *wise* ("to render knowledgeable"), hence ("to advise or guide"). The implication: a geezer knows something? But knowing becomes a way of being, a manner, a guise, a mask, hence "disguise." Maybe a geezer's "wisdom" is the result of dropping life's pretensions, one by one, his clarity and quirky character quickened in a slow motion tragi-comic, soulful strip tease in the invisible audience of a greater, animate mystery.

On Mountaintops We Are Starkly Soulful

I first saw Mount Rainier in the early sixties. I was hitchhiking back to college in Southern California after a spring visit to a friend at the University of Washington. The weather was overcast and a restless mist masked the Cascades. I was facing north on Highway 99 thumbing the remnant morning commute when the sky cleared, and I didn't see "the mountain" until I turned south to walk out of the midmorning traffic backwater. And Rainier was *there,* looming shockingly huge, an inscrutable giant, hoary preadamite elder, above the dim cacophony of the strip.

Suddenly and incontrovertibly imminent, the foreboding eminence of the earth awoke in imagination, a mysterious faintly ominous majesty, a monument honoring a force beyond my ken, a presence both familiar and strange. In that brief startled blink, Rainier seemed like the fire-darkened crown of eternity.

In the origin myths of traditional culture, a mountain embodies the archetypal beginning. The mountain is the center of the world, the navel of the cosmos. Mythologically, the mountain rises from the primal chaos of waters, marking and clarifying the murky horizon of ocean and sky. It separates the first mother and father and arrives as the first child of eternity, centering the sea, lifting up the heavens.

The mountain was the first earthly home, a place for the gods to play and the fellowship of creation to thrive. The first temples imitated mountains. The ziggurats and pyramids were sacred because they were mountain-like. At the top of the temple, at the top of the mountain, we were at the center of the earth, the place where time begins.

The montane inspiration of early temples is true. The few times I have been on mountaintops, the exhilaration I felt was not from being "elevated" or closer to heaven but from something less grand yet more fundamental. On summits, knolls, tumuli, promontories and peaks, we are most pointedly aware of our peculiar human situation, face in the cloud-scoured heavens, feet firm on rock rooted deep in the hot-hearted gravity of the planet. On mountaintops we are starkly soulful, grounded in the ancient earth, quickened in the oblivion of the sky, simple wind-shivered lightning rods of wonder.

Mountains are the bones of the Northwest Bios, the essential architecture of its salmon-haunted dream. Imagine the Puget Sound climate without the Cascades to thicken, funnel, dam and direct the wet marine weather of our latitude. Imagine our lively, unpredictable rivers without the gravitational force the Cascade cordillera supplies. Imagine our salmon-rich streams without the rattling braid of water-rounded gravel that issues from the steady wreckage of the mountain slopes.

Mountains inform all life here, are the bone of its animate body, the firmness of its character. Rainier, "the mountain" in Puget Sound vernacular, symbolizes the mountain's elemental role in the Northwest drama. "The mountain" is the regent, the lava-hearted monarch of this wet green eddy of creation.

But Rainier is not merely royalty. My spring-sudden epiphany of Rainier's eminence ineffable above the toy-like intensity and commercial anonymity of the American highway has ripened in long reverie into something darker and more fertile than I have allowed so far.

Our word *mountain* is rooted in the Indo-European etymon *men* ("to jut out, project"). This root gives us the Latin word *mons, montis,* hence our word mountain. The same root *men* supplies the Latin verb *minari* ("to project, overhang, to threaten") and arrives in our speech as *menace.*

This etymological coincidence echoes an intuition that beneath its stately repose, its unfathomably dense and weighty "jut," Rainier is dangerous. "The mountain" periodically swells with mercurial fire; storms pivot on its prominence and many people have died in its crevasses, blizzards and avalanches. Rainier is dramatic and beautiful because in our hearts it is edged in a shadowy sublimation of peril. "The mountain" is a slow-motion Tsunami of fire, rock and ice; one day it will break and blow us away. We secretly fear it the way we fear God. The mountain inspires awe and dread. We are a mountain-fearing people.

But the mountain sublimates more than our fear. The ancient Irish imagined prominent hills or mountains as "sidhes." A sidhe was the fairy abode, the place where the perennial spirits of the land abide. For me, Rainier has become a sidhe—the dwelling-place of the forgotten spirits, the fateful energies of life in the Northwest: raven the changer, cannibal woman, salmon woman, snot boy, thunderbird, the throng of personae who spoke through and for the life here and who hide now in the mountain's dome awaiting re-invitation into our desiccate commercial culture. In my imagination, Rainier shelters their natural sovereignty.

The mountain that still startles us is a fundament, a temple, the first place, a terrible power, a sidhe, the secret hive of our children's dreams.

LARVA

IN SUMMERTIME WE SWIM in our neighbor's lake. Sometimes after work in the early fall when the water's too cold for Dru or Sara Mall, I go back to refresh myself.

About twenty yards out from the dock that we dive from is an old fir snag, riddled with woodpecker holes and home for the perennial alder who sprouts, grows a few years in the rotting bark, then dies. It is the place mosquito larvae crawl out of the water to begin their eerie gelatinous transformations. It is a totem, a vertical shore, and I swim to it instinctively each time I enter the dark lake.

My ritual is to swim to the sunward side and inspect the trunk around the waterline to see what's new. One day as I hung still in the cold water of the snag shade, an osprey passed just above my head: I felt the wind of its wings—from above, a wet head of dark hair must look like a fish bloated by the sun. It's good practice to imagine one's head as food.

But the most marvelous thing that ever happened at the swimming tree was, like many transformations, small and took a long time to happen. It was late afternoon in August; I had swum to the snag and begun my perusal of its trunk when I noticed, about a hand's width above the water surface, a strange, armored insect-like creature clinging to the bark. It was the size of a small double-nutted peanut and still wet from its rise out of the lake.

Its shape reminded me of a Hudson Hornet with thirteen coats of amber lacquer, Kerouac's favorite car, a shape you might drive south or in a dream. The last Hudson Hornet I had seen was driven by a saintly Macedonian bouzouki player in L.A. It reminded me of moth pupae I sometimes unearth in the garden, and I remembered that *pupa* is a verbal familiar of the *pupil* in schools and eyes. It was a larva of some kind. Writing this, I discover *larva* was originally a Latin word for ghost or household god. Seeing it there on the bark brought back the times I tossed a log on the fire and watched a spider running the wrong way up its length. The larva was numinous as the pecking noise inside an egg. It was baby Osiris wrapped in an amber shroud.

It rested there in the setting sun, drying off. It amazed me how anything could be so still. Then in an instant its eyes lost the light and a hump bulged up on its back like a child balling up beneath its blankets in nightmare. The hump began to pulse like a fouled sail or hammered thumb, then suddenly burst and out slid what appeared to be a thin pearlescent phallus with eyes. It rested, half-emerged from its former body, now broken and dull, the light already haunting it; and I thought of the bouzouki player's deathless laugh as he drove out of the dingy gas station where I spent my youth. The creature was catching its breath, what the Greeks called *psyche*. It was calling old grandfather wind to enter it. He came and soon the newcomer moved, its whole body hearty as it left the wreckage of its water life.

It crawled a little further up the snag, following the setting sunlight. On its back were two tiny veined balloons like water wings filled with iridescent fluid. Seen closely, they were like world maps drawn by some mushroom-eating medieval cleric. With each pulse of its newfound breath the balloons stretched a little and its body darkened infinitesimally to blue. It was pump-ing up its wings; it was becoming a dragonfly.

My body began to numb from the cold lake, but I could not leave. The silver was peeling off the back of my mind's mirror and the wind eye was opening, the world was winking at me. The dragonfly followed the sun up the snag. It was a desperate race; tree shadows crossed its path like the hand of God, a deadly cold welled up in every shade. Once about two feet up the trunk a large wolf spider jumped out at him—ambushed, I thought, a pilgrim with his throat cut—but the dragonfly rose up like an unhorsed knight, opened its forelegs wide in embrace as if to say, "Welcome home, sucker." The spider wisely retreated to its lair to prey again, and the dragonfly resumed its race with the sun.

At a long arm's length out of the lake it finished its wings and waved them resolutely in the evening air. I could hear their faint hum like a mother lulla-bying a child in a far room. If night had overtaken it, the dragonfly would have awakened in the morning a wingless hawk in a land of wolves, a dud, Babe Ruth with a rubber bat. I wanted it to fly: the mind's glass clouded again with silver, I was seeing myself again and I blew what was left of my warmth towards it. Twice-born, it knew better and folded its wings to await the sun's return.

In that moment and in my memory the dragonfly is *beautiful*, beauty being the marriage of freedom and necessity. It is the *promise* hidden in the form of a stone ax head, an old bell, a salmon, or a sorrowful song. It is what the ancients called Soul.

Red Boat/Pink Buoy

For Caroline and Dorik

In this fist of dark mountains, in the mercurial shimmer of this eternal yet transient curl of sea floats a red dory, tethered to the bobbing salmon-pink knob of an anchor buoy. The leashed boat cavorts and jibes with an animate dignity, like a well-bred horse or dog, spirited, gracefully testing its master's strength. The clownish noggin of the buoy holds its place with comic tenacity; a barely souled machine, a maritime R2-D2, the plastic apprentice of a sorcerer long gone enacting the koaned, tattooed directions.

"Hold the boat."

It is such an eerie pleasure to watch them play, the buoy and the boat. They practice a manifold carousel of emotions, the genteel peevery of the captive dory so eager for the sea, its patient frustration with its idiot groom. Sometimes, absent minded, they feign escape in a concerted tideward rush but are forever reined in short by the humorless unseen anchor and its bedrock instruction.

This pantomime, the tug-of-war burlesque, masks a deeper shade of mystery. Perhaps the pale egg of the buoy, a ghostly salmon egg, is tending Taliesin's sea-worn cradle* that teeters on the small tumulus of watery shadow beneath its lapstrake ribs. And what is hidden beneath the night-blue shroud of the dodging craft? Cases of rum? A set of hand-carved oars, brand new or worn smooth by the glassy oaken labor of rowing? Perhaps it is only the tangled Gordian knot of last year's fishing gear, a halibut-stirred mess of hoochies, hooks and lures…. At sunset I imagine the boat a blood-red coffin sacred with the smiling mummy of an old Finnish fisherman, earth-brown pipe broken in his hands, the mutual clay crumbling at rest on the heavy breath of the sea.

My quixotic friends practice their soulful play "night and day" below my window, a faith that quickens my own dark blood-slick dreaming. By my witness I have learned what they play. These alluring puppets of the sea rehearse the winds and tides that tempt us all.

11/95
Sitka
Margaret Calvin's Print Cabin

*Taliesin was the shaman/bard of ancient Wales, who was found as a babe, cradle lodged in a salmon weir. It is said his cradle floated 40 years at sea before his "arrival."

Words Bear Nature's Wisdom

As a child I dreamed of finding a message in a bottle. It never happened but later I found a phrase in my thoughts that satisfied my childhood fantasy. The phrase floated up on the shore of my mind: "Words bear nature's wisdom." It was a message from the hinterlands of language, from the background of our speech. So I searched the dictionaries, the accounts of travelers in that ancient land. I studied their versions and attempted this essay, a verbal sketch of the land the message came from. Actually these speculations are field notes, life histories of a few of the local inhabitants. Imagine the words reviewed here as plants or creatures living in a place called English.

When two ecosystems meet, say the forest and the prairie, you often see a border of rich diversity and fertility; a place of increased *imagination*. The metaphor of the fertile border informs this speculation. I'm imagining language as a spoken border that bends the light of the world into our shade, *informing* that energy until what we say is what we *see*. This is an admittedly romantic notion. In the "real world" language has become a narcissistic tyrant, a tool to keep the burning world at bay. Words make *things* real when it should be the other way around; *things* make our words real. Modern messages arrive in words; we are converted in conversation, not alone on the road to Damascus. Increasingly we experience the world as a simplified verbal conception avoiding its plasticity, its heat, its color and chaos except as they approach us through words. We have turned the words themselves, once gates for the world light to enter through, into guards to ward off the world. We blind the world with words and feel guilty that our contact with the cosmos is not more direct, more sincere. We suffocate in our speech; it becomes prophylactic rather than seminal. Perhaps because language is a human event we feel that it is cultural rather than natural. But language is not ours any more than the estuary is the land's or the sea's.

Language is the fertile border. The world is in the words as we are. It's only because we don't listen closely enough that the world seems outside our speech. The world is in the words as we are; language is really a form of *introduction*—from Latin *introducer* ("to lead into the circle or house"), one echo-system to the other. Maybe words are message bearers who've been there and back, tricksters who see both sides at once; inside out one glove fits either hand. A word is a meeting place, a shelter in the woods, a *tryst,* a *trust,* a *truth.*

I see language as the record of myriad meetings between humans and the cosmos, two "natures" woven into wisdom, a fertile border, an echo-system, the meat of our nature's meeting, a skin with soul on either side, a semi-permeable membrane, a go-be-tween, mercurial, tricky and true. Language has a life of its own and words, contrary to popular contemporary metaphor, are not so much tools as organisms, evolved symbiots living in the ripe edge between nature and ourselves. Rather than oiling, polishing and sharpening our *terms,* we would do better to feed and water our words as if they were plants and animals, attend them, cultivate them, honor them, leave them be. We might approach them as hunters and gardeners rather than engineers, mechanics or arrogant tinkers. And if words are sometimes tools, then we do well to see the *life* in the tool, the wood in its handle, the bone in its blade. Words are more like game trails than machetes. The word *term* originally meant boundary. A *term* is where we meet the world. Speaking and listening well allows us access to the *informed* silence of the other side.

It's a sorry thing, but words are more often printed and read than *spoken.* We've taken words out of our mouths. The urban landscape is a riot of aes-theticized print; super-graphics, billboards, neon signs, etc., while our speech resigns itself to pale formulae of grunts and trendy catch words. Our rap becomes our wrapper: the world a product, the wrappers disposable, the product consumed. We read in silence refusing the words breath. It is only recently we took to reading in silence. St. Augustine was more frightened than surprised by his teacher who read in silence…and now we have speed reading, passing the words so fast they blur into a wall, polish into a mirror where we witness our alienation. But the world shines in the *inspired,* in the breathed, word. If we speak and listen well the world appears in the words. For instance, researching the history of words associated with books we un-cover a marvelous series of vegetative images stored in the etymons. *Etymon's* literal meaning is '"true word" and etymology is "talk about the true word." The *etymons* are the roots the words grow from, the place where the stories of the *terms* are stored, meetings remembered.

For example the word "book" is from Old English *bece* ("the beech tree"). The first books were runic beech rods. A book's pages rustle like leaves. We leaf through a book. A page was originally a trellis, words on a page like leaves on a trellis. The word library comes from the root word *lubh* that means ("leaf or tree bark"). *Script* and *writing* grow from roots meaning to scratch on bark. Trees still sway in our *terms,* old forests haunt our speech. *Speak* itself is rooted in the Indo-European etymon *sphareg* ("to sprout, to strew, to scatter"), whence our words: sparkle, sprinkle, sprout, sperm and speak. These terms are cognate, "born together," born of a common ancestor like species of finches The kinship of these *terms* image words as wet burning seeds, breath-born sprouts twisting in the light.

I see etymology as a kind of divination, a revelation of the image, the meeting recorded in the heart of the word. Record is from *re-cord,* Latin for back to heart, hence memory. A recorder is one who takes things to heart, a minstrel, a singer who played a "re-corder" that didn't use tape. Leafing through Eric Partridge's *Orgins,* the *Oxford English Dictionary* or the *American Heritage Dictionary,* we cultivate the images alive in the words we speak and read. *Read* by the way is kin to *riddle.* Because English is so modern, so smooth a tongue, the roots slide by our speech. The root images don't echo in our words. In older, less polished, languages the roots reverberate in the words; puns glisten like dark stones breaking the surface of the spoken stream. Our speech has become a blade we polish but never plow with. Our speech becomes self-reflective and vain rather than a weather-fated flowering in ancestral soil. Etymology places the word with its parent image. It makes our speech more familiar, more resonant. By the word roots we come to *terms,* the border, hear the word's heart beat recorded. In the roots of words we are at the edge, the fertile border where words bear nature's wisdom.

Language is an ecosystem; words bloom from ancient roots. We taste them on our tongues, re-inspire them with our breath. I imagine them as old beings reborn daily walking on thin air like thistledown, reminding us words are communal coals rekindled by our breath, blooms cajoled from roots by changing weather. Words can die like whales, calypso orchids or elk. What kills words? What chases them away? What finds them? Do we starve some words and nurture others? Domesticate some while others return to the wilds of the unconscious? Game trails become freeways, Roman highways become ghost-ridden goat paths. Are the Gods that the ancients saw in words really dead, or awaiting re-birth, mouth to mouth recitation, the shroud unrapped? In Latin *mater* was a venerated mother-tree. Cut down it became *materia, whence* ("material, a dead tree, lumber"). Is a materialist one who worships the dead mother?

When we miss the roots we mistake language, making up words in our heads. *News Week*-ese, Nixonese, corporate double tongue, cyber-systems gabble and psychobabble are some recent examples. True words bloom from roots, the wild roots inside/outside A false word has no echo, no resonance, no answer, no ecosystem, no family, no ghost. False words are stillborn, born without hearts and hence unable to *record*.

I like the idea of words as *persons*. *Person* is from the Latin *persona* ("mask"). In Roman theater the players wore masks that the sound, their voices, came through; *per* ("through)" plus *sona* ("sound") gives *persona*, the mask the speakers wore. Words are masks the sound comes through, persons like us. Imagine them as persons, their spelled bodies traveling through time, changing costumes (customs) in tune with the weather. Each word a pilgrim with a venerable image, a talisman close to her heart. Each word bearing a bit of nature's wisdom, seeking true sight, inspiration; the breeze that whistles through the mask, rustles in the trees.

At the border we meet the truth; ourselves and the world resolved in a word, *true*. In the heart of truth there is a tree. Truth is from the Indo-European root *deru* or *dru* ("oak or tree"). Truth's cognates are: truce, trust, tryst (now a lover's rendezvous but originally it meant waiting for game in the trees), durable, dryad, and druid. A druid is one who sees the tree. Partridge says the "truth is firm and straight as a tree." But ecologists can tell you there is more to a tree than firmness and straightness. *Trees* and *truth* are alive. (Life is from a root meaning sticky or sap-like.) A tree eats light, locks that energy in carbon and water and stores the mysterious food in the roots. In fall a tree sheds its leaves to the ground where various organisms compost (de-compose and re-compose) them into soil, *humus*. *Humus* is the root for human, humble, humility. The tree nourishes it-self on its death. The tree cycles all this energy, *informing* it. Roots feed leaves in spring; leaves breathe in light and CO2 to feed the roots and breathe out the air that *inspires* us. The roots pull minerals, broken stones, old bones, the bodies of all that dies nearby to build the tree. The heart of the tree is dead. The tallest tree is supported by its dying. Only its skin, leaves and roots are alive; its core is no longer sticky. Imagine forests of gray-skinned sadhus climbing their deaths to reach the light. In these ways a tree stores and re-stores its place. Maybe the truth is like that, a specific living mix of water, light and death. Perhaps philosophers should imagine themselves as orchardists or foresters or renegade loggers as well as architects of thoughtful edifices.

There are many trees, many truths in the human heart: *Yggradsil,* the world tree of Norse mythology had leaves in heaven, roots in hell. Yggradsil held the world together; in its shade lived the Norns, whose name means "whisperer." The Norns spin fates. Fate is from a Latin word *fari* ("to speak"). *Fate* is kin to *speech*, "coming to terms," and words as we shall see are spinners. Odin, the father of the Gods, sacrificed himself on Yggradsil. Osiris was imagined as a cedar tree. Gilgamesh destroyed the sacred forest and cursed his life. Genesis has its trees. In the *Rig Veda* the world is hewn from a tree by a cosmic carpenter. Every culture has its holy trees. Buddha found enlightenment beneath a tree and Christ was crucified on a kind of tree.

The truth is like a tree and so is language. Language imagines itself as a tree. In dictionaries we see the "tree" of language; the Indo-European trunk branching into Balto-Slavic, Persian, Italic, Celtic, Germanic, and off these branches sprout smaller branches—Frisian, Breton, Rumanian, Latvian, Urdu—and each smaller branch be-leafed with words and rooted in a special place. The whole tree shimmers in the wind, whispering. Words have roots and stems, speech is sprouting. Trees compose the soil, bear the air. Language grounds us, inspires us.

Perhaps language is a fateful tree, the leaves of our present speech absorb the light, feed the ancient roots that store the condensed images, the aeons of human weather, the rings. The health of the tree depends on the ability of the leaves to bear the light energy to the roots and the power of the roots to pull nutrients from the earth. Lastly the fruit, the bon mot, the poem, epics, the local joke, songs, new versions; the *tree* releafed again and again, turned to the weather, mendicant oak. The tree makes our world; we live in its shade.

Words bear nature's wisdom. Tracing the roots of this expression we re-emerge in other names, penetrate familiar images (*penetration* from Latin, *penes,* [inside]), blossom in other sprouts, verbiage, sparking words re-inspired, old wind in the world ash, laughter of ancient women gossiping over their drop spindles.

> **WORD:**
> Words are sources (from *surge*) of power, condensed myth (from *muthos;* speech, story), If you know someone's name, their myth, you have power over them or at least special access to them. Words were messengers of fate long before the Freudian slip. (A slip is also a twig or shoot; 'a slip of a girl'; it also means to clothe, we slip into something, sleeve, sloop, slop, slope.) Is a Freudian slip stepping on a banana peel dropped from the weird sister's picnic basket?

When we delve into the root of *word* we come to the obvious, it is from the Indo-European root *wer* ("to speak"). But philologists offer no informing image for *wer* except to hint it may belong to a large tribe of words informed by a sense of turning and spinning. So, *word* is a blossom close to the ground. When we say "words bear nature's wisdom" we mean what is spoken bears nature's wisdom. A word is one knot in the language web that echoes and re-imagines nature's complexity. From the turning and rolling in the heart of culture, to the race and running in current and course, every word is a metaphor using images to create nuanced connective meaning. The metaphor is firmed in our saying, and it is here that a clue appears that may reveal the way a word works. Saying and seeing seem to be etymological familiars; witness the similarity between the past tense *saw* ("having seen") and the noun *saw* ("a story"). Both share similar roots, Indo-European *sek* ("to say") and *sekw* ("to know"). The saying lets us see and vice-versa. Likewise the root of *diction* and a host of other speaking words come from the Indo-European root *deik* ("to point or show"). A word, it seems, is breath informed with witness; the seeing spun into saying, the sage reciting the revealing saga.

Words are an echoic web, a silk-ragged lace vibrant in a world woven by wind, rain and light; our spidery minds so nimble on its ancient net, the breathy braille of the mystery we weave, the paradoxical see-saw-saying of living. Words bear nature's wisdom.

BEAR:

Bear means to carry, to endure, to birth, to suffer, to bring. Words bear nature's wisdom. Bear's cognates are: birth, bairn, bier, bore (tidal), burly and burden. Old Norse has *bara* ("a wave, a billow"). Celtic has *inverness* for *estuary,* "a carrying in." Bear's Latin cognates give: suffer, offer and fertile. The Greek stem bears amphora, metaphor (born across) and euphoria. The image in *bear* seems to be hands and wombs: wise old midwife, storm-wracked pippin creaky with fruit. Words endure, birth and bring nature's wisdom.

NATURE:

The intrinsic qualities of a person or thing; "He was good natured." *Nature* is the order and essence of the physical universe, the "Laws of Nature." It is the outdoors, enjoying nature, reality, "the nature of things"; and lastly the processes and functions of the body, "the call of nature," coming and going. All these senses resonate in the phrase. *Words Bear Nature's Wisdom.* Inner and outer, our souls and the wilderness meet in this word, nature. Words bear our nature's wisdom. Words bear her nature's wisdom. Words bear its nature's wisdom.

But nature is not abstract, not imprisoned in the world of our notions. She, we, and it live in places, contexts. (A context is something woven together.) Nature is expressed differently all over the earth. The tree in truth may be an alder or cedar here, a redwood in Marin or an oak in England. There are a myriad of trees representing a myriad of ecosystems. What tree grows in your heart? Without a place, without some special soil, our words lose resonance; our images thin without a specific reference. Without a place words became hothouse plants grown in our heads. We become tourists riding jargon buses, viewing nature from air-conditioned comfort. Language needs a place to grow. It wants humus, compost of image and experience, rings of weather. Words are the clappers in the weather-driven bell of the world.

Nature is rooted in Indo-European *gene:* a root woven into so much of our speech. *Gene* gives us ("gene, kind, gentle, genius, kingly, innate, gonads, germinate, gingerly, kindle, and nation"). *Natio* is the goddess of birth. Nature echoes in all these words. She is a multi-visioned being, gentle generous genius in and about us. Careful speech brings us closer to her; words bear her essential wisdom.

WISDOM:
'Wisdom has two roots *vis* from Indo-European *weid* ("to see truly; I have seen, I know"). From this root we have: vision, wit, wizard, evidence, Veda, witness, idea and history. The root notion in all these words is "seeing is believing."

Dom is a suffix denoting state or condition. From its root we have Old English *dom* ("law or decree"). *Dom* is also kin to Middle English *deman* ("to judge, condemn, to doom"). (Wisdom is the verdict of sight.) Lastly *dam* is kin to *doom*. (Wisdom is the doom of seeing.) Words bear the doom in nature's vision. Words are nature's verdict, her *sentence.*

COMMONS AND COMMUNITY

TONIGHT I'VE BEEN INVITED TO TALK to aquatic and marine educators about community and commons. But I would miss entirely the spirit of community and commons if I didn't acknowledge that the heart of what you're about to hear was quickened, tempered over 25 years of conversation with my beloved wife Sara Mall and that whatever insights blossom here are borne of our communion.

A couple of years ago, Sara Mall and I traveled to Western Ireland in search of salmon folklore. The rivers around Dingle still have viable salmon runs. In fact, there is a lively little creek that runs through Dingle. Strolling by the creek one day, we noticed three old men seated on a stone bench puffing pipes and gossiping in Gaelic. I thought if anyone can tell us about the salmon, it's these old 'geezers." So I stepped up and asked the first one, "Are there any salmon in this stream, sir?" He lowered his pipe and announced firmly, "No salmon here!" "Maybe he's daft with age," I thought and asked the graybeard next to him. "No salmon here!" he replied with some irritation. Still, I could not believe my ears and turned to the third smoky sage who hissed, "No salmon!" before I could open my mouth. Still, something didn't make sense and we walked down to the docks in hope of finding a fisherman. We found one mending his gear on a tidy double-ended boat. I asked him about salmon in the creek and he echoed his fuming elders, "No salmon here!" In desperation I asked, "Do you ever catch salmon around here?" "Oh, yes," he replied, "next month the place will be full of salmon!"

It struck us with telling force that these men were part of a community in touch with the commons. Salmon were an occasion, not an idea or symbol and, more, they were a shared occasion. Community and the commons meet truly in the present tense. What those old men were saying was that it was not time for the salmon and the seeming abstract nature of my question was almost meaningless. To them, salmon were the tongue that rang the bell of home, a silvery resonance that had its time and place, a note felt and enjoyed by all.

I began salmon restoration work as an idealist. I thought the work would bring me closer to home, the natural world surrounding us. I have lived here 30 years and that sense of occasion, the storied synchrony between human community and the natural commons, has just begun to dawn on me; salmon are no longer an idea, they are a felt presence—the landscape is haunted by salmon. And as I have learned and rehearsed salmon's keystone role in Northwest ecosystem dynamics, that haunting has blossomed into a vision wherein salmon are sea-bright silver shuttles weaving our rain-green world. From marine carbon in riparian flora to winter wren's occasional pecking the eyes of a spawned-out chum, salmon are the ties that bind. Consequently, I have come to imagine that we are all threads in a mystery, water shrew, elk, slug, sinner, saint, all expressions, words the Earth is speaking, intoning a language we are just beginning to learn, and salmon are the secret grammar of that vernacular, the language the Earth speaks here.

Words are important to me. Language is every bit as ecologic as nature. We are its weather. Language has a history, and is constantly evolving; words become extinct, migrate and change their habits and habitat. Tonight I'll pause occasionally to look more closely at a word, the way you might stoop to examine an oddly shaped mollusk, or focus your microscope into deeper magnitude. Words belong to families. Words born of a single ancestor, a root word, are called *cognate,* which means "born together." *Community* and *commons* are cognate as are *commune, commonwealth* and *communicate.* These words all sprout from a single root. The oldest, deepest root is Indo-European *moinis,* which means ("gift or exchange"). The Latin branch of that root is *munus* ("a gift or civic obligation, duty"). *Munus* gives us *munificent,* "wealth making, generous." It also sprouts *remunerate,* to "pay back." When you couple *munus* with *co,* you *co-munus* ("obligatory gifting together, mutual obligation and promise"). This root sense of mutual obligation and promise is what informs community, commons, communicate, even immunity, which originally meant free from obligation, free from civic duties.

Seen from the root word perspective, the commons is nature's shared and inter-related gifts and the obligations they imply. Human community is a shared sense of gift and obligation. The natural commons is the larger community that contains and sustains human community. Traditionally, the customs and culture of human community are synchronous with and gratefully respectful of the larger context of the commons.

In traditional culture, we eat salmon and our bones eventually feed the trees that shade and feed the waters that give salmon life.

Unfortunately, we no longer live in direct contact with the commons. Our civilization has become a mechanical contraption that cruises through the commons imagining it can short-circuit the traditional obligations to the commons with cyber stretch technologies like genetic engineering. But despite our clever techno-wizardry, we cannot escape the fateful truth that human community, its vitality and survival, are grounded in the munificence of the commons. For most modern people, daily experience is removed or buffered by convenience technology from the grave and radiant poetry of the commons: alder leaves drifting down to blanket salmon carcasses, red-legged frogs hopping solitarily through the forest brush bound for a pond they cannot see, but know its exact location.

No, we no longer live in and with the commons community. We live in an uncommon fantasy, consciously separate from the larger natural surround. We count ourselves privileged to be free from nature's thrall, its mortal beauty. And yet there is something missing in the prophylactic techno castle we feel so free in. What is missing is mystery. So we love to visit the commons where it abounds. But we come as tourists, not inhabitants, our feelings born in sentiment, not necessity. We find refreshment in the wonder of diversity—the co-evolved formal beauty of the myriad creatures of the commons, their mutual obligations and promises. But we don't belong to it, no longer depend on it directly, intimately. We are co-evolving with computers, not salmon. McLuhan was ominously correct—the medium is the message.

The commons is nearly synonymous with ecology. *Ecology* comes from two Greek words: *Oikos* ("household, dwelling place"), and *logos* ("narrative, speech, talking, storytelling"). So ecology is the story of the dwelling place, the house tale. Curiously economics has a similar etymology. *Oikos,* ("household, dwelling place"), plus *nomos* ("distributor"). So economics is household management. *Economos* originally meant ("steward"). The two words are sympathetic where the steward tends an economy based in the commons.

But our house is no longer the commons; rather, it is a system of self-rehearsed machinations called commerce, an institution that has little sense of home. Western civilization has abandoned the security of being part of the story for the dubious comfort of a profit and loss statement. We now belong everywhere and nowhere.

But for most of our history, we belonged to places, the way salmon belong to streams. That is why the world has so many cultures and languages that grew contained and contexted on islands, behind mountains, separated by rivers and seas. We co-evolved in all the eco-tones of the planet and the wealth of human cultures and languages, witnesses of thousands of years of intimacy with Earth's diversity.

Our psyches, arts and languages were nurtured in the mutual obligation and promise of indigenous realms. Our language witnesses the places where we achieved our humanity. Indo -European peoples evolved their cultures in forests; we know this because our word truth traces its roots to an ancient word for tree. *Deru.* This root gives us trust, truth, truce, tryst, betrothal and tree.

The truth is like a tree: leaves catch the light, the bark protects the sap wood that circulates vitality, the dead heart wood holds the tree up in the wind, the leaves take in the light, the roots mine the ancient earth-born nutrients of the ancestors. The truth is like a tree. No wonder we troth, truce, trust and tryst in its shade.

The commons community is still grounded in places; weathers, geologies and water regimes conspire (or is it commune) to shape plant and animal communities into special ecotones over millennia. Ecotones that become dynamically complex and subtly nuanced in the local communion of community. Summer chum salmon have been returning to Chimacum Creek for at least 8,000 years. Indigenous peoples were just as loyal to places. But times have changed and people of the industrial age follow career paths, not the seasons, and in our dubious and privileged mobility, the commons have become a place to visit, not to work. Resources once dignified with sacred respect are now commoditized materials we see in board feet and pounds of oysters. Our relations with the commons resources are mediated by machines, not prayer. *Resource* comes from Latin *re-surgere* ("to resurge"). But digging deeper, we find *surge* has another root—*sub-regere* ("ruled from below"). So a resource surges back, ruled by powers hidden from view.

Our civilization has become a kind of Earth satellite, kept in orbit by the resource gravity of the commons. Yet the more we consume, the weaker the gravity of the commons becomes; someday the commons will let go of us. (*Consume*—destroy utterly by fire; hence *consumer*—neighbor, comes from a root that means near fellow-dweller.)

So in a kind of pre-industrial nostalgia, we come down to Earth to play, but not to live. Our obligations to the larger community of the commons are sublimated into corruptible, arbitrary laws rather than the co-evolved customs of accommodation and exchange. I learned last night that our state department supervising eel grass beds has ruled that an invasive species of eel grass, an annual rather than the native perennial, has been okayed as a remedial substitute in destroyed or disrupted eel grass beds. I wonder what the herring and salmon smelt who co-evolved with the perennial form of eel grass would say about that if they could.

We all sense the precarious health of the commons that support us and know that somehow we have to re-integrate our communities into the life of the commons, re-establish community, communication and communion with the commons. We have to re-synchronize our lives and livelihoods with the commons if we are to survive long term. But how? It won't happen by fiat or government regulation. Money can't buy connection. It will happen if we have a change of heart.

Your heart will one day say "don't move, stay put." The longer you stay put, the longer you are located, the deeper your experience of the local commons and the more you encourage your neighbors to form their community in and around the commons. You fly-fish for cutthroat at the mouth of Chimacum Creek, count coho redds in Fauntleroy Creek in Seattle, play poker with third generation loggers and fishers in the back room of a Shelton tavern, or read poetry in a rain-drummed crummy with tree planters on a logging road up the Dosewallips.

The first obligation of the new community of the commons is to stop moving. Communities whose populations turn over every 15 years are not liable to be loyal or curious towards the commons that sustain them. Salmon are dedicated to a locale, fir and cedar are dedicated, calypso orchids are dedicated, we alone consume the munificence of the commons without accepting the customary *co-munus*, the mutual obligation and promise everyone else abides by.

I realize staying home is an idealistic and difficult promise for us freedom-loving, mobile moderns to make. It will take a long time and persistent will to exchange our wheels for roots, to become neighbors rather than consumers. But it is not impossible!

I believe the people in this room are playing a pivotal role in evolving commons-based communities in places they love. You are aquatic and marine educators. Education comes from a Latin word *educere* ("to lead out, bring forth, rear"). You are a special combination of guide, midwife and parent, which sounds about right for the marine educators I've met. The public needs to be educated and encouraged into becoming part of the commons, to re-enter the house rather than speculating on its value.

You are part of the lucky few in this age whose livelihoods are intimate with the commons. Yours is a new intimacy; traditionally, humankind was intimate with the commons as hunters, foragers and harvesters of the commonwealth. Traditional people had common sense, a sense of shared community. They lived within their means, took enough to live in gratitude, and encouraged the larger community to thrive. Along the West Coast from Santa Cruz to Yakutat and down the East Coast of the Pacific from Siberia to Hokkaido, indigenous peoples practice many versions of the first- salmon ceremony, where the first salmon was ritually cooked and eaten by all and where sometimes the grease was rubbed on the bellies of children. Its bones were usually returned to its natal waters in the belief its spirit would tell the other salmon people to bring their gifts to local people.

Your life and livelihood in the commons is different—you spy on the commons, watching and witnessing, returning to us with news and revelations of its wonders. You lead us back to open our eyes. You are the shock troops of reconnection, the Sacajawea of re-entry to the most real work, the commons. You are trained in the methods of science to focus on the object of study, but your work is to educate, to lead the public into a deeper awareness of the commons community, to leave them curiously inspired on the doorstep of ecology. And while your science is necessarily impeccable, I'll wager that privately the creatures you inventory, survey and witness the life cycles of are not objects or even objective to you. I'll bet you love them, and because you know how they live, love and die, they have become more *thou* than *It*, perhaps even "people" in the sense indigenous people used to describe the creatures of their community: salmon people, raven people, otter people. You witness a community of *thou*(s) but, true to the scientific discipline of your profession, only share these perceptions and feelings informally with close friends and colleagues. You teach the public eco-logic and save the eco-legends for your friends and children.

Science is a powerful tool. By excluding the subjective perspective, it assembles an understanding that can be tested, shared and believed. Science is self critical and self regulatory, deepening and expanding knowledge, mapping the unimaginable complexities that compose our world. Science documents the community of the commons, the structure, chemistry and tempo of mutuality. *Mutual*, by the way, is an etymological first cousin to *community*. Science builds windows for that intimate witness where the smolt transform into youngsters, but does not instruct us how to feel about such wonders. Feelings are relative and unreliable to the scientific perspective and, hence, science shuns subjectivity because subjective imagination invites confusion. The data get sticky.

I am an artist. Our discipline is to trust the subjective because its honest loneliness invites inspiration as well as confusion; it's worth the risk. But science is right to be suspicious of unfettered subjectivity. Left alone in a boundaryless self-referenced perspective where every thing is relative, subjective creativity becomes absurd, produces art with minimum apparent meaning and long footnotes. But imaginative witness in context (*context* means "woven together" as in ecotone novels or communities), subjective imagination contained by a real place is self-sorting and self-organizing. The containment of context encourages the imagination to depict relations, articulate a world that is related, not relative. In context, the imagination's witness is tempered and tuned by generations until the commons is represented and understood as a story. The eminent Rumi scholar Colman Banks once remarked something to the effect that "story is as essential to culture as facts are to science."

The stories quickened by the subjective imagination in context and told over and over in that same context come to embody the truth of the tree rather than the truth of fact. But the truth of the imagination, disciplined in context, and the truth of science are not oppositional, but resonant. Native Americans lived with salmon for thousands of years and evolved stories that are uncannily sympathetic with the latest findings of ecology. Local cultural ethos is explicit, science's ethos is implicit. The difference between native culture and science-based civilization is that native people lived in the light of their understanding while we quibble in the shadows over the legal and proprietary implications of our knowledge. The necessity for the human community to reconnect with the commons is crucial, and you are leading the public towards that connection.

The stakes are high and time is short. The public needs to be informed but, even more, the public needs to be inspired. I think it is time to meld objective science with a dash of subjective art, to encourage art and science to tryst occasionally behind the tree of truth. I don't mean researchers should do water colors or write poems. But I can imagine you educating the public from another perspective—a viewpoint that encourages and quickens the restorying of the commons, because it is through stories that it will truly be resolved. Community completed by communion.

How could it happen? I imagine a marine educator explaining the ecology of eel grass scientifically, laying out the food webs, the nutriment cycles, the crucial role these play in salmon and herring life histories and the complexities of life forms dependent on eel grass, and offering a metaphoric story that begins, "It's like." A story that condenses and personifies the dynamic of the eel grass community into a narrative explicit and memorable—an artful, articulate rendition that inspires listeners and makes them part of the story. A story that reminds the listener that we are members of the commons, even if we pretend we are not.

Or a marine educator could conspire with a writer or artist, meet behind the tree, and commune, communicate until they find the story, each perspective an aspect of the subtle "joinery."

Another example: Jeff Cedarholm has been documenting salmon-based nutrient transport and salmon-based food webs in Northwest ecosystems for years. His work needs the transformative energy of a marine educator—a poetic conspiracy to condense his work into an artful story that can charm our collective heart back into salmon sanity.

It is through the artful articulation of the commons that we rediscover communion. The commons and its creatures begin to re-inform our vernacular, our language relocates in locales, finds its metaphoric strength and depth in the resource world, not the ephemeral homeless cleverness of technology.

The resonance between human community and the commons won't happen overnight. It will take stubborn retelling and refitting the stories by generations of people willing to stay put for the transformation to occur. But remember we are in the inevitable tow of ecologic gravity, not economic haste. Ecosystems spiral slowly forward in time, evolving, and if they are to survive, economies will have to eventually synchronize with the ecologic tempo.

My hope is that artists and scientists can *co*-operate to change the focus of human endeavor from wanton commerce to careful community. (*Focus* is the Latin word for *hearth*, "the place where the local gods dwell." Ainu people passed all game meat into the house through a window directly in front of the fire so the resource, the power hidden behind the veil of flames, could see they were treating its creatures well.)

Community and commons naturally coalesce into culture. We don't enjoy real culture. We consume fragments of culture decor floating in a torrent of distraction and entertainment. We pretend to the boredom and ennui of royalty with our demands for continuous novelty. True culture is place born. *Culture* comes from the Latin verb *colere* ("to till the soil, to walk around a place"). Its past participle is *cultus*, hence ("culture"). *Wheel* is a close relative of *culture*. Culture turns with the seasons, it is a mobius striptease revealing and concealing in its turning. The soil is the past, the ancestors—all that went before, salmon, trees, parents. We turn the soil into the light so it may bloom. Each day is a marriage between the past and future. What we call ourselves, human, comes from Latin *humus*—*our* name means soil born.

In ancient Ireland there was a belief in a creature called the salmon of wisdom. This mythical creature was said to live in the well of Buan, the great nature goddess. The well was surrounded by magical hazel trees whose fruit fell into the well and fed the salmon who lived there. Sometimes a "pretender," an innocent future king of Ireland, would chance upon the well and the all-powerful Buan. If he could survive her riddled invitations and win her heart, they consecrated his kingship by making love by the well. The well echoed their passion and overflowed into the five rivers of Ireland and the salmon escaped to return to bless the unexpected with wisdom.

In one village an old wise woman once dreamed that a man of her village named Finn would catch one of the salmon and by tasting of its flesh would become the enlightened avatar/king of Ireland. Of course, every family named their first son Finn, but after some generations and no luck with the wise salmon, the practice subsided and Finn became just another name.

Well, there was one lad who believed he would catch the salmon of wisdom and set to fishing on the grassy banks of the Boyne (Buan's river). He became an adept fisher and eked out a living supplying the village with trout and salmon. Finn, in his old age, knew all there was to know about catching fish and one rosy evening when he saw a dark swirl near the far shore, knew it was a large salmon and cast expertly just ahead of its eddying wake. His knowledge paid off, for when the salmon broke water to shake the fly, there was the salmon of wisdom, scarred, draped in torn nets, pierced by broken spears, adorned with all manner of hooks.

But Finn was old and weak and the salmon, huge and powerful, began to pull him down the grassy bank into the river. In desperation, old Finn cried out, "Help me, help lest this great fish drown me!" And who should be walking along the river that evening but young Finn headed home after a day playing hooky from school.

So young Finn ran down and helped old Finn pull in the great fish. Exhausted, the old Finn said, "Young friend, thank you and if you'll be so kind as to cook this salmon and give me the first bite, you can have the rest to take home to your family." Now young Finn was from a poor household and knew this fish would bring him great credit in his parent's eyes. So young Finn built a spit, cleaned the fish and began to cook it. But as the fire was a little too hot, the great fish began to blister and young Finn, in absent-minded care that the fish not look poorly cooked, reached out with his thumb to pop the blistered skin. Well, the fish was hot and greasy and young Finn's thumb was sorely burned and he thrust it in his mouth to cool it.

Sucking his fish-greasy thumb, young Finn could suddenly understand the language of birds, could hear the song the grass was singing to the rising breeze and knew why the old Finn wanted the first bite; this was the salmon of wisdom that the village wags joked about.

So young Finn confessed his mistake to the elder Finn, who graciously allowed that he had become wise enough in his 65 years by the Boyne and that it was fated that a young, powerful man should become Ireland's savior. And so the young Finn became a great hero. But whenever he was faced with a great decision or intractable problem, he had to suck his thumb to see through to the truth.

Smart, Not Wise

Eighty-two years ago a warrior from the Mount Lassen region of Northern California stumbled, starving and half mad with grief, into Oroville, Calif. The sheriff found him huddled by a slaughterhouse corral fence, surrounded by barking dogs and curious townspeople. The genocide against his people had ended 30 years earlier. But the last survivors of his tribe—the warrior, his mother, uncle and young niece—had survived as watershed ghosts. They swept their tracks, cooked on smokeless fires and ate only salmon, small game, roots and plants.

Despite their considerable skill at secrecy, they were discovered by a power company survey crew. Fleeing in honest fright, the uncle and niece perished fording a flood-swollen stream. The warrior carried his invalid mother to a secret place and cared for her until her death a month later. For the next three years the warrior lived a grief-stricken nightmare, bereft of family, terrified of the whites closing in around him. Finally, in a kind of suicide, he burned off his hair in a traditional show of mourning and stumbled into Oroville to meet his fate. Luckily, the sheriff contacted University of California (UC) anthropologist A.L. Kroeber and the Yahi warrior was taken into his care.

Kroeber, more than any other person in California, knew who this man was—a traditional Native American traumatized but unvanquished, untouched and unchanged by industrial society. Kroeber knew a few Yahi words and won the warrior's confidence through his respectful treatment. When Kroeber asked the warrior's name, the refugee answered simply, Ishi. *Ishi* was the Yahi word for "man" and being a traditional person, Ishi could not reveal his true name. He was known as Ishi until he died.

Ishi went with Kroeber to the UC-Berkeley museum in San Francisco and worked as a caretaker and anthropological informant until his death in 1916. Before Ishi's death, Kroeber asked him his opinion of modern society and its "conveniences." "Smart, but not wise," was Ishi's laconic answer.

121

—

Reflecting on Ishi's perception of our "way," I discovered that much of our daily speech reflects his perceptive distinction between wisdom and smarts. For instance, we now say "bottom line" instead of fundamental or basic, thereby shifting the metaphoric heft of the concept of essential grounding from foundation to commercial credit. The origin of this spoken value has been transferred from the good earth to a ledger.

Although we seem fatefully inclined to smartness rather than the wisdom Ishi embodied, our language is grounded in a tradition of wisdom similar to Ishi's and etymologies (origins of words) offer the same practiced witness. Many word roots (etymons) reflect an older, more balanced relationship between humans and nature.

For thousands of years, humankind perceived the natural world as part of the family, worthy of care and respect. Nature was a thou, not an it. The hyper-rationalism of the 18th century and Newton's now obsolete but nevertheless brilliant reduction of nature to mechanics "dehumanized" the natural world and made possible the industrial revolution. Nature de-souled, explained in reductive mechanical terms, allowed its denigration into property and encouraged its abuse. The "mechanization" of nature allowed us to wantonly exploit the natural world. Our understanding and relationship to our home places changed from a neighborhood of generational responsibility to one of proprietary power over speculative assets, "property," real estate. It's a fine line between alienation and abstraction. We abandoned our homes to make a "killing."

—

The rise of extractive, reductive capitalism and its obsession with property and profit embody the opposite of Ishi's imagination wherein the world is an assembly of *thous* not an inventory of *things*.

It is only in the last 200 to 300 years that we have become so obsessed with property, profit and power. For most of human history, despite the profligacy of elites, culture was closer to Ishi's wisdom and the roots of our words reflect this.

Consider our word material. It sprouts from the Latin root *mater*, which meant ("tree trunk") as well as ("mother"). Cut down mater and you produce *materia*, Latin for ("lumber") or, put more directly, ("mother-substance"). *Mater*, the mother tree, is still haunting us; she is the dark echo of our materialism.

Ishi's distinction is also evident in the words we use to express "verity." Presently, we discriminate only slightly between fact and truth. Truth has more natural weight than fact, though we'd be hard pressed to explain why. A look at these words' roots confirms our intuition. The basic sense of fact is something done. The root is Latin facere ("to make"), hence ("factory, fact, feat, fashion"). There is an ambivalence in fact's sense of itself. How was the fact produced? A fact isn't really firm until we know its history, its agent or author. Some facts have multiple agents and authors. It is only the shuttering of our curiosity that allows us to polish facts into data and input. Is a bee a hive being, a future queen, or a device of a flower to fertilize itself? The "bee fact" is simply the radiant nexus of all those stories.

What about truth? Truth grows from the Indo-European root *deru* or *dru*. *Deru* meant tree; its progeny are ("tree, truth, durable"). *Druid* (*dru* plus *vid* ("the one who sees the tree, trust, truce and betrothal"). In the imagination of our ancestors the truth was like a tree and so it is! The truth and trees are alive. A tree "eats" light and transmutes its mystery through the alchemy of chlorophyll into carbon and water. It stores the mysterious food in its roots. In fall, a tree sheds its leaves to the ground where an infinity of organisms compost (compose) them into soil, humus. (*Humus* is the root for ("human, humility and humble").

———

The tree (durable truth?) cycles all this energy, informing it. Roots feed leaves in spring and leaves breathe in light and the carbon dioxide waste of other creatures to feed the roots and breathe out the air that inspires us all. The roots pull minerals, dissolute stones, old bones, the bodies of all that dies nearby to grow the tree (truth?). The heart of the tree is silent, resinous and dry. The tallest tree is supported by its still heart; only its skin, leaves and roots are truly alive. In these ways, a tree (truth?) stores and restores its place. The life of a tree vitalizes the metaphoric heart of truth; irreducible, it defies our attempts to cut it up and cook it into data, without succumbing. You amble around the truth; you don't have the truth, you meet it; like Buddha you dream in its shade.

Words and their roots reveal older patterns of relationship. Etymology is really an exquisitely condensed folklore that precisely witnesses the character of our experience. Wisdom is stored in the roots and dictionaries are full of deep dreams. But moderns ignore roots. War and depressions have taught us that money makes a slippery world. We slide away on it, homeless.

Ishi admired the cleverness of our machines but saw through them. He liked locomotives because they were huge, dreamlike and scary and he was a warrior. But he didn't like shoes. He said they broke his contact with the earth and hurt his feet.

Curiously, *smart* comes from an Old English word meaning to feel pain, sharp pain, hence able to pierce, hence smart, hence shrewd, clever. In contrast, *wise* buds from the Indo-European root *widein* ("to see"). One sees, one knows. This root yields ("evidence, witness, wisdom, provide and wizard"). *Smart* and *wise* represent attitudes. Smart is sharp. Wisdom is remembered witness. Wisdom is the care for a true story; smart is dividing the spoils.

Tradition tells us the smart should serve the wise. Rather than dividing the spoils we can begin to witness the truth here, smell the cedar and the fir, and re-enter the assembly of Thous.

STUMP

There is a fir stump near our old well by the creek. I cut it for firewood fifteen years ago. It isn't large, maybe eight inches in diameter and was growing in the shade of a larger fir until I cut it. I didn't pay much attention to it after I turned its trunk to wood. Then years later I passed it carrying water to the barn and I noticed it was healed over, like the stump of an arm missing its hand, a concentric cumulus of cracked bark, a scar armoring the end of its empty reach.

Fir trees don't usually heal over, so I made a point of showing it to the local DNR forester. He explained that the mycorrhizal roots of trees intertwine and actually communicate chemically, and that the larger tree (still green and standing) probably sensed the wound to the smaller tree and "instructed" it chemically and nutritionally to heal. Which it did. It now appears as a handless arm that's lost its grip on the light, or has it? It shows no sign of rot; it's still rolling bark over the old cut, still alive in the shade of its mentor whose own green hands continue to catch and share the day.

HOMECOMING

IN THE EARLY NINETIES OUR LOCAL salmon restoration group undertook a stock restoration project to rebuild the summer chum runs on two East Olympic Peninsula streams, Salmon and Chimacum creeks. In September, fisheries agents trap chum spawners in a weir and take a percentage of the eggs. These eggs are "eyed up" at the Hurd Creek Hatchery in nearby Sequim and then turned over to us to incubate in a small hatchery we built on a tributary of Salmon Creek. By protecting the eggs, we can boost the egg-to-fry survival by almost one 100 percent and hopefully build up the run. We watch the eggs until they hatch, and then feed the fry to a certain size and release them to their sojourn in the sea. Seven volunteers alternate checking eggs and fry daily from November to late April. We are committed to this project for at least ten years. We hope to rebuild the Salmon Creek stock first, and then transfer Salmon Creek fish to the chum-barren Chimacum system.

One clear January day I was at our little homemade hatchery checking water temperature and flow, alert for the early hatch that sometimes occurs in a warm winter. I lifted the lid on the incubation barrel to check on the 46,000 eggs, the progeny of twenty wild chum hens, supported by black screened trays, vibrating and rolling delicately in the smooth rhythmic shade of the water flow. It is always a little eerie peering into this watery womb, and I leaned down to study the eggs' opalescent glow. I was trying to decipher what the subtle changes in egg color meant; I was wondering at the dark sentient density of their eyes. These eggs can see and that day I had the uncanny sensation that two eggs in particular were watching me. They followed my motions, rolling and twisting to "see" me—it was unnerving. As I closed the incubator lid and began to write up the daily report, I had the eerie intuition that those eggs were the eyes of the watershed, venerable and rejuvenant in the same moment. It was as if 8,000 years of watershed experience, the bio-logic, the patient wisdom of Salmon Creek, was coiled in those two vigilant eggs.

Driving home, my hatchery encounter brought to mind a Fraser River Salish story I'd read years before. In the story, Swanset was married to a woman who was one of the Sockeye Salmon people. Newlywed Swanset lived in his wife's village and ate with them. Each evening his mother-in-law would come up from the river carrying a salmon in her arms like a child. She cleaned and cooked it in a respectful way and called Swanset and her daughter to eat. Swanset's wife carefully washed her hands before eating and cautioned Swanset to do likewise. The old matron warned him not to break the salmon bones but to lay them carefully to one side. At meal's end, the mother-in-law gathered up all the bones and returned them to the river. Each evening upon returning the bones and ambling up form the river, stately in the twilight, she was followed by a young boy who rollicked in circles around her. The Sockeye People were glad to see the merry lad; he was vivid witness and a celebration of the rightness of their way. Swanset was curious about the miraculous child, and so one evening he kept one of the salmon bones hidden in his mouth. When the boy appeared that evening he was lame, unable to dance and leap. Angry and suspicious the villagers confronted Swanset. His father-in-law, the chief, threw him to the ground, retrieved the bone and healed the crippled youngster, who joined them by the fire.

The genius of Native wisdom is to return the bones—complete the circle and honor the gift by giving back. It is this spirit that blossoms so beautifully in the image of the boy frolicking around the dignified grandmother. Our genius, the industrial trick, is to crack the circle, mine its wealth and move on. In our contemporary story the boy doesn't dance but preens sulkily in the rearview mirror of a car, radio blaring, while the grandmother is singing down by the river. The boy is afraid to leave the mirror's enchantment and celebrate her miracle.

Maybe it's as simple as this. In a consumer society, sustenance is a spare transaction: we buy fuel to hurry into the future. For traditional people, food is sacramental and eating is often an act of remembrance and hope. We can't go back to the past and we can't follow our present course into the future. We need a new-old way of looking. Musing on the profound difference between our quick-witted consumer culture and the sustained wisdom of traditional neighborhood cultures stirs a childhood reminiscence worth retelling.

When I was a child I loved marbles. I had a big wooden box full of cat's-eyes, aggies, "puries," clay marbles from Mexico, stone marbles from North Carolina. When spring came and the ground had dried, recess would find us racing across the schoolyard to an old oak tree in whose shade we would draw our circle on the cool clay ground and play.

We laid out our risk marbles, picked our shooters and lagged to see who would shoot first. Every marble had a meaning and each of our marble bags held an anarchist chess set. The marbles had histories and personalities. Some were heroic, some beautiful, some old and chipped. But all possessed a kind of marble soul. You rolled these marbles around in your hand like a strange seed, a fossil bone or arrowhead.

We played ferociously and hilariously. The best player was a raven-haired girl named Marcia who hooted and leaped, talking to her marbles like fish in a stream or make-believe grandchildren far from home and in danger. It was a mythic drama we enacted in those dappled green days, a kind of fateful dreaming that required all the qualities adults were coaxing in and out of us in their formal way—daring, skill, practice, strategy and imagination.

But there was a minority of players who didn't see it as poetically. These players would inevitably propose allowing "steelies" into the game. Steelies are polished steel ball bearings from three-eighths to three-quarters of an inch in diameter. Steelies were a technic fix. They required only good aim and a strong thumb, and whoever went first with a steelie usually won. Other marbles couldn't budge them, and the risk marbles and shooters that were our imaginary friends became fodder in a bottom-line game—win at all costs. Every year we voted steelies out; our game was a theater, a magical circle, not a get-rich-quick scheme. Ever since then the phrase "losing your marbles" as a metaphor for insanity has had a special resonance for me. I think it is the same deep seriousness of that childhood initiation into the natural heart of culture that inspired thoughtful communities from Japan to Northern California to take responsibility for their local salmon runs. The circle in the clay resounds with the cycle broken, and further with our forsaken spiral into the bottom-line solipsism of steelies.

Governments and most businesses play with steelies. They must—we hold them accountable to standards of efficiency, not to beauty or soul. They probably won't save the salmon, because they are distracted by the perennial cacophony of special interests and the pursuit of profit. It is the locals, the neighborhood people, with small circles and vernacular marbles, that may be the truest and most useful constituency for the salmon. What better agents than ourselves to revive our region's salmon runs? We are the natural kith to their kin. We marvel at the miracle of their return, argue over their health, and rise early to troll and mooch for them in the dark testy weather of the North Pacific. We ceremoniously savor their firm yet delicate flesh, subtly cooked in a myriad of local and family recipes. In smokes, spices, sauces and glazes the salmon is the soul food of the North Pacific. And while they delight our senses the salmon also represent us in a profound and heartfelt way; they are the precious mettle of our watersheds, they embody our home places. Salmon are the deep note of our dwelling here, the silver soul of this green bell—steelhead, sockeye, coho, chum, pinks, and kings.

But be warned against restoration romance. Salmon restoration is a paradox more salted with irony than leavened with heroics. Because we assume responsibility does not mean we're in control or will succeed. The salmon know what they're doing. The mind of the "leaper" is tuned to geologic time, and our entropic, superheated civilization may be a minor perturbation in their world. I can imagine salmon of the twentieth millennium spawning in the moonlit rubble of the Kingdome. Perhaps the question for salmon is how big will civilization grow before it consumes itself? For us the question is, can we get back in synch with the salmon cycle in time to bank our fires in a suitable hearth. Restoration work is really reinhabitation; community building with all the "neighbors."

If you try to restore salmon to your watershed you soon discover the neighborhood is haunted by salmon. The gravel road I drive daily was built decades ago in the middle of a stream. It was the easiest way. Once a small salmon-rich brook, it now trickles schizophrenic in ditches on either side of the road. The brook's cycle, the flow, pulse, quality and quantity of this watersheds' water has been drastically altered not only by misplaced roads, but by conversions of forest to pasture and dwellings, short-rotation timber harvest and impoundment of this once-spirited rill in ponds that make fish passage impossible. Even if the cutthoat, steelhead and coho that once homed to this unnamed stream could follow its scent home, they could not navigate the tattered threads of its unraveled waters. Following the salmon home is labyrinthian daunting work.

Revisiting the history of the salmon's decline in our neighborhoods is depressing, but stream work and habitat revival is full of high-spirited comradeship and the small epiphanies of recognition and connection that bloom when what you've done actually works. I recall the chance witness of a coho parr leaping into a culvert we laddered for fish passage two summers ago. I remember the glee with which we greeted one small fry in a rill that we reconnected to its main stream, and also a couple of cutthroat fingerlings nestled in the scour pool behind one of the boulders we'd placed in a stream that was down-cutting because it had lost structure (wood and stone) and couldn't dissipate its energy. Discrete, vivid moments like these weave us into place. They reconnect us to the complexity and wonder of the natural world, rekindle our imaginations, and edge us away from the unconscious thrall of consumption and back into the quickened drama of creation and community. Restoration then becomes restorying the landscape with tales of its essential beauty.

Imagine a Thanksgiving dinner of your great grandchildren a hundred years from now. In the center of the table is a bright silver salmon locally caught and cooked in the practiced way of long enjoyment and reverence. At the end of the feast there will be a simple ceremony—a long walk to the creek with neighboring families, each with a wooden bowl of salmon bones, to return the remains to the waters of their creation in gratitude and respect. Perhaps there will be mention of the ancestors, if that is who we decide to be—the old ones who stayed put, who gave the salmon shelter in their hearts and who found their own way home.

5 • FOCUS

My friends used to laugh at my old Latin teacher, Mrs. Gleeson, a hunchbacked crone who clacked her false teeth in furious punctuation when she read aloud from Caesar's *Gallic Wars.* But I secretly loved her because she revealed that words have souls or at least roots, and are alive as you and I. She taught us that if you honor the heart of a word, your imagination feels a deeper gravity, a richer calling.

We learned that *focus,* a word with Etruscan roots, before its current meanings of clarity, intensity and efficiency, originally meant hearth. Focus was the dwelling place for two families of deities, the Lares, local gods of landscape and nature and the Penates, gods of the house and home. These deities of the inside and outside world were embodied in the hearth fire, *focused* in the flicker of our mortal witness. We worshipped them in the baked mud house of the hearth. So originally, *focus* was not a synonym for *precision,* but a name for the local prescient mystery resurrected daily by a simple spark and our spirited breath.

The hearth is the heart of a household. Households are confirmed in marriage. Marriage is a shared and consecrated hearth, husband and wife focused together, kindling a common fire, sharing warmth, chopping wood, cooking and bathing, attending the perennial surprise of children, tempering their vivid heat into focus, honoring the local gods inside and out.

Every morning husband and wife blow the dark, dream-dim coals of wonder back alive, back in focus.

Each day we sweep up the hearth's ghostly ashes for the garden, lay the day's fire and listen to the ancient gods of our common life whisper from the flames dancing in witness before us now.

Winter Greeting

The machine won.
Its clawed mind
caught us all,
enthralled.

Yet somewhere
in the pale dawn dark
of the snow-still forest
a woodcutter cradles
a frozen axe blade in his hands,
warming its bitter edge
against the daily work.

Sifting

A true secret
is passed secretly

      like night rain
      falling between the terrible stars,

and if not secretly
then humbly,

      the fire-folded loaf of stone
      waiting unbroken in the road.

And if not humbly
then honestly,

      a blind man dancing
      to heart's old dream.

And if not honestly
then kept,

      secret

a dark bird
silent in the royal dusk.

Loki

Fire,
the licking secret hidden in wood,
makes our amulet words,
molding its laughter in our two-eyed echoes.
Doubt it?

What is it then that edges us and all we see?
Not dreams nor time,
but some grim flickering force
a bright imperfect hunger.

Lasting Light

The bright poets
strike their tempered steel
against the flinty world,
sparking a brief sacrificial radiance
that blesses life's tumult in its fall.

The shadow poets
sing another way;
at home in the abiding silence,
they feed the haunted hearth
their weathered wood.
Blowing on the storied coals,
they coax forth a smoky
longer, lasting light.

Drunk Song

This road is gray cotton
for my eye's slow wound.

This car is full of
bees and babies.

My heart is a poisoned arrow
fired aimless in the night.

Names

"Star thistle, Jim Hill Mustard,
White tops, Chinese lettuce,
Pepper grass, the names of
Things bring them closer."

—Robert Sund
Bunch Grass

Names are ghosts
that lead us home, home to old houses
full of working spiders
and webs taut in shadow and light.

Names are winds;
small breaths
that open doors and close them.

They are honed lenses
breaking light
that otherwise would blind.
They are tools to make time.

Names are fate's osmotic flesh,
living cells robbing meaning from the sun
and dying in their time.
Names are a lame man's curse on dancing.
They are weird skins dropped on moving mysteries.
They are flayed seals barking
in a circus far from the sea.

Names are gypsies knocking
at your back door selling charms
and hexing your home if you do not buy.

They are odd winks,
incisions, wounds
and weddings;
they are the two-timing sweethearts
of our souls.

Post-modern

When the garden
is blooming mechanical flowers
the parents become scarecrows

Bangor

When it comes
it will be quick.
Your old high school sweetheart
will be making tuna sandwiches
for her kids
in a stucco house in Poulsbo.

Young Ed from work
will be getting his hair styled
at the mod barber's in Bremerton,
hating the thought of swing shift,
envying the old men playing pool
across the street.

That strange girl from days past,
you could never figure her out,
but it hurt when your buddies
mocked her strangeness.
She will be scuba diving in Hood Canal,
looking,
just looking.
Your oldest boy
will be reading the P.I. on the ferry,
home for the weekend,
thinking about quitting school again,
troubled by problems
neither of you see.

When it comes
it will be quick.

The heat will peel
your old sweetheart like a grape.
Light blinded
she searches bravely
for her moaning children.

Ed is cut in half
by plate glass,
an infinity of surprise
in the barber's mirrors.

And that girl
you could never figure out,
that strange girl,
Barbara,
will be carried by a wave
into the tree tops
speared by a burning fir.

Another wave will catch your boy.
The red hot ferry will hiss
as the wave wraps its cold fist around it.

Where will we be
when it comes?
It will be quick.

We are coaxing it home,
wooing it down into the strike zone;
the perfect pitch,
the last out,
inevitable.

Stirring a bad dream with easy lies
we will awake in flames.

Ghost

In daylight
a ghost is a winter tree,
leafless in the slanting storm;
it's green gone underground
dreaming with wren bones
and the echoes of summer's lost songs.
This wraith is not dead…
there is no death.
The simple gravity of spring
tows its pale sun-gyred hunger
back to life,
up into the day to catch its light,
to coil seed and cast it,
to haunt doom's dark wealth
with bloom.

But in the deceptive rest
of night's oceanic silence,
a ghost is the iridescence
of light's long fall refracted
in the mortal waters of our moment;
its broken radiance redressed in colors
so we know it's real.

People

Waiting for the Seattle ferry
in the exhaust and impatience
and two crows drop
like black tattered books from the gray
unlettered sky, fold the ragged
pages of their wings and strut,
bluffing each other
for a piece of stale bagel.
"Crow people," I mutter,
surprised at their humanity.

Science

Science is the plain view of wonder;
the unrelenting record of a world
whose secret compass is your heart.

Science is not life but life's echo scripted,
the constantly revised notation of a symphony
impossible to perform or conduct.

Science is logic's spy in the burning palace of awe.
It is the well spoken secretarial ghost of the real.
Churched in reason's dry witness;
it is the unblinking keen of worldly love.

Return

Fear, booze, the rat-faced brawls,
the bluffing wit and broken promises...
the bitter sweet wounds of women
turned to salt...

Born to water
but afraid to swim
I polished the spook-toothed sea
into a circus slippery mirror.

Each morning I comb
my unruly vanities into style.
The actor's waxy ruse masquerades as meaning
and the mask fattens in the clownish smile
of intrigue and false imagination.

In my murky mirror
love is a stillborn secret
drowned in the leaden paint of my lies.
Finally the mirror fails its fatal fascination and falls,

shattering into a desert of splintered light.

Beware this is not death;
but death's refracted keen,
her note.
Rooted naked in her stark call
I may still climb the apple-breasted trees of time
and list at last the laughing birds of innocence.

I will let her patient gravity
sift myself as simple soil
and invite the dark to whisper;
to invite my soul to dream
that the ghost green, seed-cracking shoot
of my life may wave above earth's grave wisdom

tapping at the empty sky to rain.

Snow

We waited for the snow
the way children wait for sleep.

It came falling in the darkness—
ringing the air in mystery,
a thousand moths in a black stone bell.

It was the final snow of winter,
and we danced in it like wounded birds
       and laughed.

It was a snow of revelation.
It was the cloak of a ghost
wrapped close enough to see.

6 • SURPRISE

urprise: 1. to encounter suddenly or unexpectedly; 2. to take or catch a person or creature unawares; 3. to cause someone to feel wonder, astonishment or amazement. These senses derive from Latin *super-prehendere:* ("to take from above"); through French *surprise* (past participle of Old French *sorprendre:* ("to take from above"). One cannot help but think of eagles, hawks, owls and shrikes; sharp-clawed hunters or, more distantly, "rapture," seized in the fierce embrace of wonder or love, *carried away.*

EPILOGUE

FISH TICKLING

FISH TICKLING IS A KIND OF SECRET surprise, the capture of wary prey under water by means of a subtle invisible caress, a subliminal seduction wherein the prey wakes up suddenly in another world. Fish tickling is an ancient skill, no tools, nets, hooks, weirs or spears, just your own hands and intuition quickened in a deft concordance of silent sensitivity.

My friend Les Perhacs can tickle fish. I saw him do it once. We were drifting down the Duckabush River in wetsuits and snorkel masks while the summer chum skirted by in their funereal calico wedding regalia. Les was the leader of our little band of novitiates, pilgrims, variously astonished witnesses of the river's radiant clarity and its mysteriously clued crosscurrents of yellow, green alder leaves and the bruised ardor of the chum salmon.

We stopped to rest at a pool edged with great ice-rounded boulders and fringed with sword fern, alder and cedar. The rest of us sat silently reflecting on what we had seen. Les crossed the pool and was standing with his back to us facing the rock- and fern-ledged bank. He began to edge slowly up and down in the currents below the overhanging bank. He moved the way a carpenter moves to check the plumbness of a wall or a dowser moves over a vein of water, a sort of slow-motion short slip-stepped jig trying to line up something subtle but intensely real. He kept his hands below the water and beneath the bank searching the river shade. Back and forth, slowly up and down the bank he danced; then he stopped dead still except for a slight lingering motion of his elbows. It was as if he were playing an underwater piano or were a blind man weighing precious rare eggs to determine their fertility. All the while Les did not look down; his head tilted back just slightly, all his attention focused in the dark liquid shadows around his hands. It looked like he was trying to remember something. Then he stopped entirely, stark still, expectant and keen as a seedling turning to the light. Now he held his arms tight against his waist the way you might hold them to carry a sleeping child and turned in a slow motion arc to face us. He was beaming with glee as he slowly lifted his hands out of the river to reveal a sleek sun- dappled steelhead who for a moment was as still as our witness, then woke to our world's burning air and flipped shaking into the leaf-scaled rill of last year's rain and was gone. Les's laughter leavened and confirmed our amazement.

Years later I asked him how he did it. He said as a boy he learned to hypnotize birds by gently running his finger from the crown of their heads to the end of their beaks. Later, night diving off the coasts of California and Mexico, he taught himself to steal into the dark world of rock-laired fish, miming the water's feathery flux with his fingers, barely brushing their throats and bellies, slowly coaxing confidence in his water-rippled touch, muting their instincts with subtle insistence till they accepted the dreamy cradle of his hands and let him lift them where he would.

Imagine if we were on the other side of the tickle. What river are we in? What is tickling us, thimbleberry blossoms in the nether-world? What strange air will we awake in? Life is rife with surprise.

Selected References

Campbell, Joseph. *The Masks of God: Primitive Mythology.* New York: The Viking Press, 1959.

Curry, Robert. "New Directions Needed for Agricultural Research." In Truck 18. St. Paul: Truck Press, 1978.

Partridge, Eric. *Origins: A Short Etymological Dictionary of Modern English.* New York: MacMillan, 1966.

Smith, Robert Leo. *Ecology and Field Biology,* 2nd ed. New York: Harper & Row, 1974.

Sund, Robert. *Poems from Ish River Country.* Washington D.C.: Shoemaker & Hoard, 2004

Watkins, Calvert, ed. *The American Heritage Dictionary of Indo-European Roots.* Boston: Houghton Mifflin, 1985.

TOM JAY WAS BORN IN MANHATTAN, KANSAS in 1943. His father's military and corporate careers necessitated frequent transfers—Mississippi, Alabama, Tennessee, Utah, Nevada and California. After dropping out of college in the mid-sixties, he wandered the world for a couple of years; stowing away on a cruise ship to Europe; working in an Icelandic cement factory and on a Danish farm. Upon his return, he discovered his life's calling as a bronze caster-sculptor. He came to Washington State to finish his education and graduated from Seattle University with a BA and an MFA from the University of Washington. He moved to Chimacum in 1969 and built and operated Riverdog Fine Arts Foundry until 1995. For the last 25 years, he has assisted his wife Sara Mall Johani in engaging the community imagination in place-based culture through art, festivals, educational adventures and salmon restoration projects.